Secrets of the Gardens

by

Pre-Construct Archaeology

Published 2009 by Pre-Construct Archaeology Ltd
Unit 54
Brockley Cross Business Centre
96 Endwell Road
Brockley
SE4 2PD

ISBN 978-0-9563054-1-1

Printed by Henry Ling (Dorset Press) Ltd, Dorset

Secrets
of the
Gardens

Archaeologists unearth the lives of
Roman Londoners at Drapers' Gardens

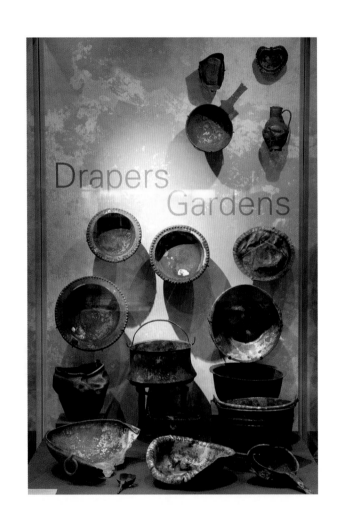

Contents

Contributors	vi
Foreword	vii
Demolition & excavation	1
The Walbrook Valley	2
Remarkable preservation	4
The early Roman period	8
Ritual & religion	14
Reclaiming the upper Walbrook	18
Buildings AD 120-250	20
Trade & industry	30
Animal bone	38
Diet & environment	42
Literacy & writing	46
The late Roman period	50
The hoard	56
Medieval & later	66
Drapers' Hall & gardens	68
The new building	72
Acknowledgements	75
Select bibliography	77
Picture credits	79

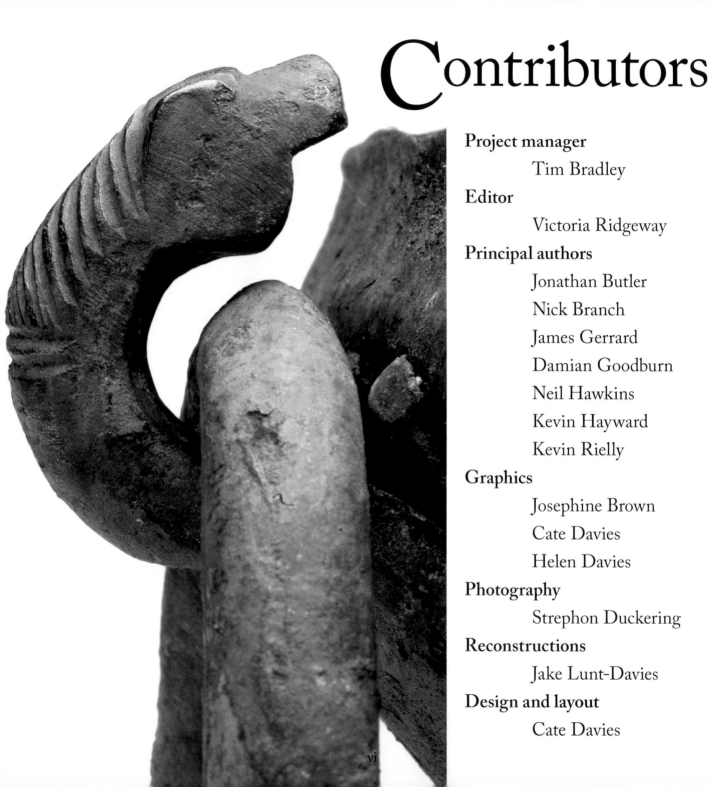

Contributors

Project manager

    Tim Bradley

Editor

    Victoria Ridgeway

Principal authors

    Jonathan Butler

    Nick Branch

    James Gerrard

    Damian Goodburn

    Neil Hawkins

    Kevin Hayward

    Kevin Rielly

Graphics

    Josephine Brown

    Cate Davies

    Helen Davies

Photography

    Strephon Duckering

Reconstructions

    Jake Lunt-Davies

Design and layout

    Cate Davies

Foreword

by Sir David Lewis, past Lord Mayor and current Alderman of the Ward of Broad Street

Archaeology and development in the City of London have a long and sometimes chequered history. Archaeological investigations can often be a costly and time-consuming frustration for developers, producing results that can be perceived as less than important. However, every so often a site comes along that changes everything, when the archaeological discoveries make such an impact that everyone on site, developers, contractors and archaeologists alike are enveloped by a joint feeling of excitement. Drapers' Gardens was such a site.

In an area of the City of London that was so wet and unsuitable for occupation in the medieval period that it was turned over to gardens rather than buildings, a lost suburb of Roman London was discovered where craftsmen, traders and shopkeepers lived alongside the very river that was later to cause such problems. One of the many challenges of the redevelopment was to safely demolish the 1960s Seifert Tower, whilst archaeological excavation took place below. But, if you were to stand on top of the rapidly diminishing tower during demolition, you could look down and see spread out before you the traces of a Roman road, flanked by timber-lined channels with the framework of buildings and yards clearly visible alongside. The many fragments of pottery, leather, butchered bone, the woodworking tools,

coins and jewellery bring to life those early inhabitants of this City who lived and worked in, or travelled through, this damp and uninviting suburb.

As this publication shows the site is in many ways exceptional. Drapers' Gardens was the largest excavation in the City for almost a decade and the particular soil conditions of the Walbrook valley contributed to the remarkable preservation of remains. These include an enigmatic early timber trackway, carved timber water pipes, an almost complete oak door, a small cemetery for the burial of babies and a bear skull, perhaps that of an animal used for entertainment in the nearby amphitheatre. But it was perhaps the hoard of vessels buried in a late Roman well that drew the most attention. The copper-alloy bowls and buckets gleamed like gold as they emerged from the depths of a murky, dark, damp well.

Steadily, piece after piece emerged and archaeologists and demolition contractors alike stopped to stare in amazement.

Yet, these are just pieces of the story of this site. Many of the individual artefacts were retrieved almost as well-preserved as the day they were lost or disposed of and will be a source of study for years to come. It would appear that the Gardens have finally divulged their secrets.

We at the City of London Corporation are pleased that the developers - Canary Wharf Limited and Exemplar Properties - allowed the excavation process to take its due course, even though the pressures on them to continue with their works were immense.

Alderman Sir David Lewis, MA, DL

View across the city towards St Paul's Cathedral.
The Seifert tower can be seen on the left being prepared for demolition.

Images on preceding pages:
ii   Coin of Marcus Agrippa.
iii   'Perlrandbecken' or pearl edged bowl, part of a fourth-century hoard of objects found in a well.
iv   Display of the Drapers' Gardens hoard in the Museum of London.
v   Moulded glass boss from the lower part of a jug handle, in the shape of a Maenad's head.
vi   Detail of zoomorphic escutcheon from a copper-alloy hanging bowl found as part of the hoard.
vii 'Perlrandbecken' or pearl edged bowl, part of the hoard.

Demolition & excavation

Beneath the bustling streets and buildings of the City of London, financial capital of Britain, lie archaeological remains which reveal that this 'square mile' has been an important settlement, albeit one with changing fortunes, for the best part of 2,000 years since the establishment of *Londinium* (Roman London) here shortly after AD 43. Two millennia of building and rebuilding has resulted in a very different landscape from that which greeted the first Roman invaders and settlers, but it is just that process of redevelopment which enables us, as archaeologists, to gain glimpses into the story of our Capital's rich and varied past.

The site at Drapers' Gardens on Throgmorton Avenue was previously occupied by one of the tallest buildings in the City of London, a tower designed by Richard Seifert, who was responsible for such iconic buildings as Centre Point and the Nat West Tower (now renamed Tower 42), and built between 1963 and 1967. Once planning permission was granted to redevelop the site it was recognised that two challenges would have to be met. First the demolition of the tallest habitable building yet attempted in the United Kingdom would have to be accomplished with all its attendant problems. Second the archaeological remains, which were known to have survived beneath the building, would have to be excavated. A strategy was devised that would allow the existing buildings to be demolished whilst at the same time enabling safe excavation and recording of the archaeological remains. This was achieved by excavating the eastern part of the site whilst the central tower was demolished and then returning to site once the cantilevered base of the tower was removed to dig the western side.

The Walbrook Valley

John Stow in his Survey of London written in 1598 described the Walbrook thus "this watercourse, having divers bridges, was afterwards vaulted over with brick, and paved level with the streets and lanes wherethrough it passed; and since that, also houses have been built thereon, so that the course of Walbrook is now hidden under ground, and thereby hardly known".

The natural topography of London has changed dramatically over the years due to natural causes and human intervention. Many of the tributaries that feed the Thames have been controlled and culverted, surviving only in sewers beneath the City streets. The site at Drapers' Gardens lies over the confluence of three channels of one of these 'lost' rivers of London, the Walbrook. The river has long since been covered over and built on and exists only in drains and sewers but was once a major feature of the Roman and medieval city. The Walbrook rose in the vicinity of Hoxton and Shoreditch and entered the City to the south of Finsbury Circus, bisecting the capital before meeting the Thames just to the west of Cannon Street station. Nowadays the river survives in the street name 'Walbrook' and the boundaries of many of the central City wards define its former course.

Archaeologists have for convenience split the river and its valley into three zones; the upper, middle and lower Walbrook. Each zone is characterised by very different facets of the river. The site at Drapers' Gardens lay within the upper Walbrook Valley, which was originally marshy and consisted of a series of small tributaries which joined to form a single channel in the middle Walbrook. The streams of the upper Walbrook are still relatively poorly mapped with each excavation in the area adding new data. The present investigation has provided important information regarding the location of at least two of the streams as well as details of how these were controlled by the Romans.

The Walbrook Valley

Head from a statue of Mithras, found in the Walbrook Valley.

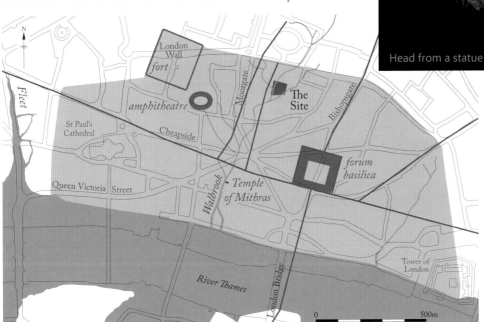

It was in the middle Walbrook part of the river that one of the most important Roman finds in London, the Temple of Mithras, was discovered in the 1950s.

The river was used as a dumping ground for much of its history with many unpleasant industries carried out along its course. Some of the deepest archaeological remains in London are found along the Walbrook where channel deposits survive at a depth of over 8m below the current ground level.

3

Remarkable preservation

The modern City of London conceals one of the great archaeological resources in Britain. Two thousand years of occupation has led to a thick build up of archaeologically-rich deposits. Unlike redevelopment today when all traces of previous buildings are removed to make way for the new, the Romans and later inhabitants of the city would demolish buildings, spread the debris across the area and then start building again. This has led to a continuing build up of deposits with the earliest material at the bottom and the latest at the top. Archaeology is the science of the excavation of these archaeological remains, of necessity in the reverse order to which they were laid down. We damage and destroy the remains of the past every time we dig a hole whether it be for a rubbish pit, a well or the foundations of a new building. Since the medieval period, on most sites in the City this process has led to large scale damage to the Roman remains beneath.

At Drapers' Gardens whole building plans, drains and channels survived more-or-less intact.

From the Victorian period onwards the construction of deep basements destroyed many sensitive archaeological deposits. Thus on most archaeological sites within the City of London it often takes a great deal of imagination and sometimes a leap of faith to produce a ground plan of Roman structures.

However, at Drapers' Gardens this was not the case. The site had been subject to late Victorian and twentieth-century development which resulted in the removal of the latest Roman and medieval layers, although there was relatively little damage to the lower, and thus earlier, deposits. But there were exceptions. A series of small concrete piles (pictured left) had been driven into the ground and, of course, the tower of the 1960s building had removed all archaeological remains from the centre of the site. Nevertheless, the ground plan of many of the Roman buildings, especially those on the eastern side of the site, could be easily seen.

On most archaeological sites the remains and artefacts that are found are most often those that are the most robust and able to survive the ravages of time. Buildings constructed from brick or stone are much more likely to survive than those built from timber for example and inorganic artefacts such as pottery, brick and tile will often make up the bulk of the finds from a site. However, these remains often afford a very disjointed story; only the wealthiest and most important structures were constructed from masonry in the Roman period.

4

Nineteenth-century building works in the City frequently uncovered amazing Roman finds. A watercolour (above) of 1848 shows Roman remains exposed during construction of the Coal Exchange in the City of London.

A timber rake head, *c.* 30cm wide, with iron tines (right) is testament to the astonishing level of preservation.

The majority of the buildings were constructed from clay and timber. Often the timber baseplates on which these walls were built and posts driven into the ground beneath to provide stability survive as nothing more than voids or stains in the soil where the timbers have decayed. Many of the everyday objects that were used by the inhabitants of *Londinium* were made from organic materials such as timber, cloth and leather which do not often survive.

Copper-alloy 'toilet set' comprising a scoop, which may have been used for either cleaning out ears or for taking cosmetics from pots, a pair of tweezers, used for getting rid of unwanted hairs and a fingernail cleaner.

A badly corroded iron key from a Roman site in Chichester (right). Using x-rays we can see what the key may have looked like (far right). Conditions at Drapers' Gardens allowed objects such as this copper alloy key (left) to be preserved almost in the state in which they went into the ground.

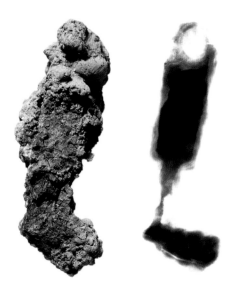

At Drapers' Gardens wet conditions caused by the presence of the Walbrook streams, combined with a lack of oxygen, resulted in remarkable preservation of objects such as fragments of wooden and shale furniture, the wooden handles of tools, leather shoes and metal objects. Over 1000 finds such as wooden writing tablets, coins, tools, writing implements, a complete door and most notably a hoard of metal vessels were recovered from site, many in almost pristine condition. But the waterlogged nature of the soil also meant that there was good preservation of the timber piles, baseplates and even wattlework that made up the buildings themselves together with timber-lined channels and drains made from bored-out logs (see page 25). The wood survived so well that the relics of ancient carpentry techniques could be easily identified. The survival of the timber baseplates allowed individual rooms within buildings to be determined and even a complete wooden floor survived in one building. An enormous and diverse assemblage of rare woodwork was recovered, which is clearly internationally important in the Roman world.

But the name of the site is another clue to why the remains were so well preserved. The use of the area as the Drapers' Company's gardens for over 300 years meant that there was little disturbance to earlier Roman deposits. Even where the basements of the 1960s buildings had removed the floors and walls of the late Roman buildings the piled foundations had survived beneath allowing the location of the walls that had once stood above to be determined.

This brooch in the form of a sitting cockerel is a well-known, though uncommon find. Brooches were worn in Roman Britain to signify many aspects of life, such as where you came from and your status and position within society. This type is thought to indicate that the wearer was a devotee of the cult of Mercury.

Leather sandal, one of many recovered from the Drapers' Gardens excavations.

The early Roman period

Following the Roman invasion and subsequent conquest of Britain in AD 43 the town of *Londinium* was founded. Built *c.* AD 50–55 during the reign of the Emperor Claudius the city began its life in the area of Cornhill, around modern day Fenchurch Street, Lombard Street and Gracechurch Street. By AD 60 a clearly planned street grid extended from Cornhill in the east and Ludgate Hill in the west, crossing the Walbrook Valley. The uniformity of the town layout could only have been born of a conscious and organised effort. The Roman Empire had by then a well established pedigree in town-planning rivalling any new town in Great Britain you may visit today. Although thought originally to be a military town, *Londinium* quickly evolved from the confines of a military outpost to become a thriving commercial centre and port. The town was now alive with merchants and businessmen, buying and selling goods arriving from the port on the Thames waterfront

A reconstruction of London in AD 60 as it may have appeared from the northwest, by Peter Froste.

and then redistributing them onwards to other towns and the more remote parts of *Britannia* (Roman Britain). By AD 60 it would appear that the town, the fastest growing in Britain, was destined to become an important and influential commercial and administrative frontier town.

It was during these early boom years of *Londinium* that sudden and dramatic events drastically altered the nature of the Roman province. In AD 60 a revolt against Roman rule swept across the southeast of the province. Led by Boudica, Queen of the Iceni (one of the indigenous tribes which the Romans had conquered) the revolt was brutal and bloody. The Iceni, hailing from East Anglia, rose up with other local tribes who shared similar grievances against the Roman rulers. The timing of the uprising could not have been planned better - the Roman Governor at the time, Suetonius Paulinus, was on campaign in north Wales with most of the province's army. Boudica and her forces faced little opposition as they spread across the southeast of the province.

Once Paulinus got word of the revolt he hurried back from his campaign and quickly put paid to the rebellion, which culminated in Boudica's death, probably by suicide. When the dust had settled *Camulodunum* (Colchester), *Verulamium* (St Albans) and *Londinium* itself, the three most important towns of the province, had all been razed to the ground; the Great Fire of 1666 was not the first conflagration to devastate London.

The town was consequently rebuilt and eventually became the capital of the province, and an important administrative and economic centre, as it continues to be to this day and it is here in the aftermath of the Boudican revolt that we pick up the story of *Londinium* at Drapers' Gardens. The earliest archaeological remains recorded were a series of timber logs lain alongside each other 'corduroy' fashion, forming either a simple track or some kind of causeway or embankment; the logs being used to spread the load on the clay that lay underneath.

Coin of Marcus Agrippa recovered from the ditch south of the corduroy. Most likely struck between AD 37-41, this was probably lost before the death of Nero in AD 68.

Such structures were usually used as foundations for trackways, roads and even ramparts in wet and waterlogged areas such as the Walbrook Valley and this trackway could have borne the weight of wheeled vehicles. The individual timbers were carefully split out of straight-grained, oak logs up to *c.* 3.5m long. At first a possibly prehistoric date came to mind due to the low level, simple construction and parallels in trackways from prehistoric peat bog levels. Then typically Roman straight edges and a few Roman finds were made. A number of logs were dated via dendrochronology (tree-ring dating) and several were dated very specifically to the spring of AD 62, just after the Boudican revolt.

Could this structure be part of the reclamation and reconstruction of *Londinium* in the aftermath of the revolt? The date of its construction would suggest so. It clearly played some role in the rebuilding of the town, possibly even defining a boundary at the northern limits of the city.

The relatively simplistic technique involved in the woodwork of this structure is unusual. Despite its definitive dating it is atypical of Roman woodwork encountered previously across London. Such woodwork would normally be attributed to native British workmanship. Could it be possible that the Romans employed local craftsmen to aid in the construction of this structure? Such a possibility isn't entirely implausible, especially given the circumstances involved following the sacking of *Londinium* during the revolt.

Timber corduroy structure. The oak logs are closely set alongside each other creating a trackway.

A ditch lined the timber corduroy to the south, with a larger channel to the north. On the northern bank of this man-made channel four small timber boxes were recorded, three of which contained the decayed and fragmentary remains of infants. Burials of human remains were a strictly organised affair during the Roman period. Laws stipulated that adult burials had to be located outside the limits of any town or city; burial grounds tended to be alongside roads leading out of the settlement.

In London cemeteries developed in the area of Spitalfields and Finsbury Circus amongst others, just outside the city walls. Infants on the other hand were often treated with less respect and their remains are frequently encountered in a number of what we today would think unusual places, such as in ditches, rubbish pits and channels. Whilst our modern-day values might see such treatment as abhorrent and against every moral code we live by, during the Roman period such things were accepted. A certain ritualistic element could also sometimes be attached to such remains.

Infant and neonate burials found below the foundations for buildings and floor surfaces are archaeologically interpreted as 'foundation' deposits - potential offerings to the gods prior to the construction of a building or settlement of an area.

In this light the apparent reverence involved in the burial of the infant remains at Drapers' Gardens makes them unusual. Care and attention was clearly paid to their interment within the timber boxes and their subsequent positioning in the ground, atypical to the Roman norm. Even more curious was the careful positioning of a whole timber door laid flat next to one of the burials. Though the preservation and survival of organic remains across the site was unusual the presence of a whole timber door is astonishing and this, in combination with the infant burials alongside the channel, clearly has some kind of significance. Someone cared enough about these infants to treat them with respect in their journey to the afterlife and while the exact circumstances behind this may never be known, it remains a curious and enigmatic archaeological find.

Plan showing the earliest two phases of Roman remains uncovered on the western half of the site.

N

palisade enclosure

burials

door

channel

corduroy

ditch

0   10m

The remains of an infant buried within a timber box. The remains were very disturbed and decayed, but this infant appears to have been aged somewhere between two months either side of full term. A further two oak boxes were also found used in a similar way. The boxes had clearly originally held other items and were reused - one was an oval bentwood box very similar to 19th-century examples, a rare find of Roman date.

Key and lock plate recovered during the excavations (right).

An infant burial alongside the intact timber door laid flat alongside a channel (below). Note the inverted amphora within the channel. Is this door simply a reused timber structure that forms a convenient platform on unstable ground from which to bury the infant dead, or does it have a more symbolic role?

The joinery of Roman buildings such as doors and window frames has very rarely been found, so the excavation of a complete ledge and plank door was a particularly rewarding moment in the project. This is the more complete example of two such simple doors found in Roman London. The door was made of three oak boards held together by four oak cross battens fastened with iron nails with the tips hooked over. At 1.71m tall by 0.93m wide it was wider, and considerably shorter, than a standard modern internal door. Radially split boards were used, as they shrink and expand only about half the amount of sawn planks with changes in the weather. Along one edge of the door a planed strip of oak had been nailed that was longer than the rest of the door and stuck out at either end, acting as a simple pivot - such a door is termed 'harr hung.' There were traces of a lock with an L shaped key, which had been crudely removed before the door was reused.

11

Timber fence pales forming a palisade.

The simple trackway appeared to only be in use for a short time. An enclosure fenced off with vertical timber planks (pales), known as a palisade, was constructed probably around AD 70, cutting through the corduroy structure. Only two small sections of this enclosure survived, one of which had a post for a gate or doorway at its western end. Unfortunately potentially the most important and most interesting area of this enclosure, the interior, was completed destroyed by the construction of the 1960s Drapers' Gardens tower.

The timber planks were all radially cleft - an ancient prehistoric technique in which logs were split in half and each half in half again and each quarter in half etc. Here they were mainly split into $1/16^{th}$ or $1/32^{nd}$ sections. Romans used such material for rather specific purposes, often where weather resistance was required.

These pales had bands of iron nails suggesting that they were fastened to three horizontal rails, which must have been fastened to larger posts at intervals. The best preserved pale was 2.21m long suggesting a height above ground of about 2m, way above the heads of Roman Londoners who were on average considerably shorter than today. The whole structure was very substantial showing that it was intended to keep out unwanted visitors and the wind. It must be borne in mind that the memory of the Boudican uprising would still have been fairly fresh – such a palisade would also have been capable of withstanding almost all projectiles such as arrows and spears.

Domestic fence pales were also found fallen in the roadside drain in later deposits but these were noticeably much smaller and thinner.

Uniquely at Drapers' Gardens many metres of palisade were found with the bases of the timbers preserved *in situ*. Additionally two palisade uprights, or pales were also found reused in a later revetment, both of which had rather blunt spear-shaped upper ends and broken rotted bases where they had been set in a trench in the ground. The evidence of early Roman activity here came as somewhat of a surprise as this area was not thought to have been settled so early in the Roman occupation, due to the wet and marshy environment of the Walbrook. It provides us with new information about these early years of *Londinium* and its surrounding environs showing that settlement activity in one form or another began here as early as AD 62, around ten years after the fledgling town saw its beginnings around the area of Cornhill.

Trajan's column (above) in Rome and other sources show us that the Romans built palisades around forts and similar locations but well-preserved examples have not been found in Britain.

Reconstruction of AD 70 palisade.

doorway

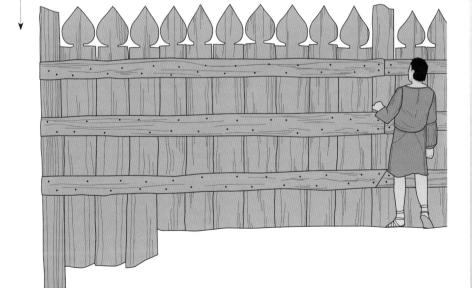

A bolt from a military ballista, a remnant from the Boudican revolt? Recovered from the ditch south of the corduroy structure.

Ritual & religion

The deities worshipped in Roman London were almost as diverse as its inhabitants. Alongside the Graeco-Roman pantheon the indigenous Iron Age gods were worshipped and exotic deities were imported from as far away as Egypt. Religious intolerance in this pagan society was rare before the rise of the exclusive monotheistic Christianity in the fourth century. Everyday life in *Londinium* would have resonated with the sights and sounds of these pagan religions. From temples and religious ceremonies observed by the many, to an individual worshipping household gods or calling on the gods to sanctify an oath or punish a wrongdoer, religion was ever-present.

In AD 306 Constantine the Great was proclaimed emperor at York. His belief in monotheistic Christianity led to many people converting from paganism and by the late fourth century there were many Christians in Roman Britain. This bowl was found in the 1920s close to Drapers' Gardens at Copthall Court. The 'chi rho' symbol engraved into its base is one of the earliest symbols of Christianity and shows that the new religion had gained support in the Walbrook Valley.

Relief of Mithras slaying the Astral Bull from the Walbrook Mithraeum, one of the most famous sites in Roman London. Mithras was an eastern solar deity who was worshipped by men, particularly in the army. Theologically Mithras represented the triumph of good over evil and was associated with the worship of Sol Invictus (the unconquered sun). The solar monotheisms had much in common with early Christianity.

For many years archaeologists have argued about religion in the Walbrook Valley. For some, the Walbrook was a watercourse imbued with religious significance and a focus for rituals that we, at a distance of almost two millennia find hard to comprehend. Others argue that it was little more than an open sewer, foul and choked with noisome refuse. The excavations at Drapers' Gardens have thrown new, if equivocal, light on this question.

The most straightforward evidence for the inhabitants' religious beliefs comes from fragments of small pipeclay figurines – little statuettes of gods and goddesses. These figurines were probably used in household shrines as objects of individual and family worship.

Small pipeclay figurines such as these were mass produced in moulds in northern Gaul and transported all over the western empire. These statuettes probably derive from small household shrines. At Drapers' Gardens the Matres, three mother goddesses (as seen here), and Venus, the goddess of love, were common.

Tazzae and triple vases are peculiar vessels that often occur on temple sites and at cemeteries. The tazzae may have been used as incense burners but the function of triple vases remains elusive.

Perhaps the most exciting evidence for ritual activity is a small piece of seemingly unexciting lead (pictured below). It is pierced by two holes, as if it had been fixed to a wall with nails, and scribed into the soft metal is the word 'noxious'. This is a type of object known as a defixione. In the Roman world you could seek the gods' help for anything. You may have asked for an easy labour during childbirth, or success in a business deal.

Other evidence for ritual activity comes from a large number of seemingly deliberately damaged objects. Styli (Roman pens) and toilet instruments often seem to have been bent and some intact pots were found with holes carefully drilled in them. This damage can be considered as ritual killing. In many societies objects dedicated to the gods are deliberately broken as part of the dedication ritual and this may be what was happening with these items.

One of the most striking finds from Drapers' Gardens was a sculpture of a female head, probably that of a sphinx, found in a second-century pit. Sphinxes in Greek mythology were guardians of the dead and it is therefore likely that this sculpture once belonged to a funerary monument. The sphinx may have formed just one part of a much larger roadside monument or may have been incorporated into the fabric of the cemetery wall.

Alternatively you could have a malevolent intent, cursing an enemy or the lover who had jilted you. The defixione was meant to be attached to a wall, perhaps in a temple, or perhaps to property owned by your enemy and the words on it would cause your enemy harm. This little piece of lead shows that someone at Drapers' Gardens believed in the power of the gods on earth.

The gods worshipped in Roman London were as diverse as the city's inhabitants. This inscription from Southwark mentions the god Mars-Camulos – a combination of the Classical Mars and the 'Celtic' Camulos, both gods of war.

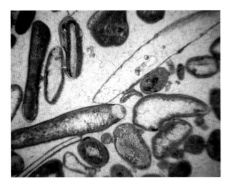

Photomicrograph of the stone used in the Drapers' Gardens sphinx.

Some of the stone types from Drapers' Gardens are distinctive enough to be identified by eye but for the limestone used to carve the sphinx and other fine-grained rock types, microscopic analysis is required. A tiny stone sample was obtained from the sphinx and prepared as a thin-section. The sample was cut with a diamond saw, mounted on a glass slide, embedded in coloured resin and ground. It was then compared with outcrop samples prepared in a similar way to identify the geological source of the stone. This showed that the oolitic limestone used to carve the Drapers' Gardens sphinx was Middle Jurassic 'Bath-stone' from the South Cotswolds.

An artist's reconstruction of the female head. Her hair is swept back in four wide strands on each side of the head which join at the back, forming a heart shape on top of the head, a hairstyle which was popular in the second century. The head juts out too far for a natural pose if this were a human figure, suggesting that this didn't come from a simple statue. Her hair style and pose resemble those on a sculpture from Colchester (left) which shows a sphinx with a female head, eagle's wings and lioness' paws guarding a human head.

As the Roman population could only bury their dead outside the town, it seems likely this came from a cemetery just to the north of the town wall within a few hundred metres of Drapers' Gardens.

17

Reclaiming the upper Walbrook ~ the first & second centuries

By the end of the first century AD *Londinium* had recovered from the ravages of Boudica and was once again a thriving town, growing and expanding beyond its original confines. As the population grew there was continued expansion outward from the original central core of the town and it was only a matter of time before the area of the upper Walbrook Valley would be formally settled. Although the environment of this area was not ideally suited to stable settlement the Roman expansionist machine remained undaunted.

To address the problems of the marshy and wet nature of the area the Romans began a system of reclamation by infilling the natural streams and then importing earth and gravel to consolidate and raise the ground. Integral to this process was the control of the various Walbrook streams. The Romans' knowledge and skill in woodworking meant they were able to divert the streams down artificially-created ditches. These ditches were lined with wood using horizontal timber planking set on edge, held in place by upright timber posts, known as piles.

Effectively this process canalised the various streams, not only once but numerous times: as old structures collapsed, when decisions were made to divert the course of the streams' flow, or as it became necessary to raise the ground level adjacent to the channels to counteract the risk of flooding. Thus multiple phases of these timber pile and plank structures, known to archaeologists as revetments, were recorded across Drapers' Gardens, controlling and diverting the Walbrook streams. At the same time, over a period of around 20–30 years the level of the ground was raised as much as 2m. So, over time, the channels became both deeper and narrower. It seems hard to imagine the ground level we walk across on a day-to-day basis steadily rising over such a short period of time but this was precisely what happened from the late first century to the early second century. It was clearly an organised and structured event involving the importation of mass material, which was lain down across the area consolidating the surface.

This organised reclamation and consolidation of the area allowed the ever-expanding town of *Londinium* to encroach on the area of Drapers' Gardens.

Multiple phases of timber revetted channels and associated building timbers under excavation.

Roller-stamped and combed box-flue tiles and a rare column tile (top) were found, brought into the site as hard core. These were keyed to allow the addition of plaster and would have carried hot air through the walls of earlier high-status masonry buildings or bath-houses.

Running virtually north–south through the site was a road, constructed from heavily compacted gravels, built over the hard-core dumped across the site as consolidation material. Usually such Roman roads would have ditches running alongside them draining off any surface water, in this case the timber revetted channels diverted the Walbrook streams alongside the road thereby simultaneously controlling the water flow and acting as roadside drainage ditches. The late first century dumps, deposited to raise the ground level prior to the structural development of this area, contained wall plaster decorated with elaborate lozenge and floral designs (right). Rather than deriving from any buildings on the site this material would have once belonged to the interior walling of more affluent residences further afield.

19

Buildings

AD 120–250

It was only a matter of time before buildings themselves sprang up alongside the road. Although many of the more prestigious buildings in *Londinium* were constructed from stone, the majority were timber framed. Usually, on archaeological excavations, the timber beams that make up the frame of a structure have long since rotted away leaving only traces of the long thin trenches known as 'beamslots' within which the timber frames would have been set. These would provide the main archaeological evidence for a building. By contrast, at Drapers' Gardens the majority of the timber frames themselves survived, providing detailed information about the structures they represent and the techniques involved in their construction.

The remains of buildings varied greatly but were all based on forms of timber framing with sill beams resting on clusters of timber piles, which had to be used to spread the weight of buildings because of the soft wet ground. On sites in areas where building stone is readily available the sill beams of Roman buildings were often raised up on low stone walls. However, the sill beams of most buildings in Roman London were set at ground level where they would have started to slowly

A range of timber framed buildings under excavation. A small domestic hearth, lined to either side with tiles, can be seen in the room in the foreground.

rot over 15 to 20 years or so. Most of the latest timber buildings on the site only survived as lines of clusters of foundation piles, features that dominated many views of the site during the excavation. Other smaller excavations in the area have shown that once fully waterlogged Roman deposits are now drying out and decaying as a result of modern building works. It is extremely unlikely that a large site as well preserved as Drapers' Gardens will ever be excavated again in London.

| Construction of the road and its associated roadside revetted channels c. AD 120 | Erection of the first timber framed building on the eastern side of the road AD 129 | A large complex of buildings to the east of the road, complete with fresh water piped under pressure and a courtyard area c. AD 160 | One of the two major branches of channels east of the road is blocked off, making way for a new building c. AD 200 |

AD 120   AD 130   AD 150   AD 200

The Antonine Wall in Scotland is built AD 138–142

City walls built around *Londinium* c. AD 190–225

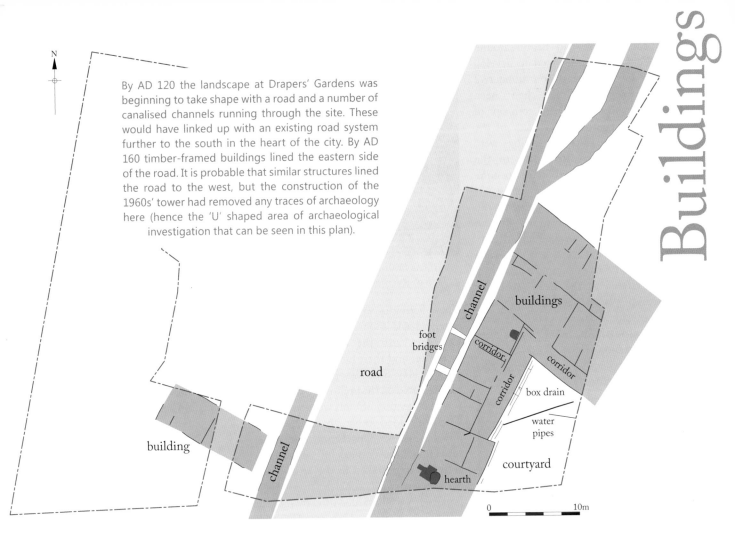

By AD 120 the landscape at Drapers' Gardens was beginning to take shape with a road and a number of canalised channels running through the site. These would have linked up with an existing road system further to the south in the heart of the city. By AD 160 timber-framed buildings lined the eastern side of the road. It is probable that similar structures lined the road to the west, but the construction of the 1960s' tower had removed any traces of archaeology here (hence the 'U' shaped area of archaeological investigation that can be seen in this plan).

N

channel

foot bridges

road

building

channel

buildings

corridor

corridor

corridor

corridor

box drain

water pipes

courtyard

hearth

0   10m

The site layout shifts to one large multi-roomed strip building dominated by two ovens after AD 200

The site layout changes again with fragmentary buildings located all along the eastern side of the road including a masonry structure to the north. The remnants of a complex of structures and an associated timber-lined well are erected along the western side of the road AD 250

AD 210   AD 230   AD 250   AD 270   AD 300

The 'Third Century Crisis'. Civil war, invasion, political instability and economic chaos AD 235–286

Septimius Severus in Britain AD 208–211 campaigning north of Hadrian's Wall, dies at York

Accession of Diocletian, usurpation in Britain of Carausius and Allectus AD 286

Allectus defeated by the legitimate emperor Constantius I, London saved from being sacked AD 296

Once construction had begun around AD 129 the area continued to develop at a fast rate. By AD 160 a number of timber-framed buildings had been erected forming one large complex of buildings along the eastern side of the road. Some remnants of buildings were recorded on the western side of the road and it is reasonable to presume that the western side of the site would have been as intensely occupied as the eastern. Previous excavations in the area of the Walbrook valley had already demonstrated that this was a centre for industrial activity, almost certainly directly related to the close proximity of a readily available water supply. The buildings at Drapers' Gardens were rather modest affairs, home to a number of craft and industrial activities, such as tanning, butchery, horn working and textile manufacture.

Vertical timber planking blocking off one of the timber revetted channels.

These activities would have taken place in the back rooms and yards of the buildings with the craftsman, artisan or worker and their family also living in the property. Small shop areas were also often located on the premises. A large and varied collection of tools were recovered. These included knives, hammers, files, punches, hooks, chisels and whetstones reflecting the range of day-to-day activities undertaken in the area. Much of the everyday rubbish from these buildings was discarded directly into the Walbrook stream, which ran alongside the road. From an archaeological point of view this furnished us with a rich assemblage of artefacts providing invaluable information about Roman activities. However during the Roman period this would have been a dirty, damp and smelly environment.

Imagine the remnants of a rotting carcass of a discarded sheep lying in a ditch just outside your house! Although horrifying by modern standards this may have been an everyday occurrence in the Roman period.

A typical Roman timber box drain (left), made like an elongated box of sawn oak planks nailed together with a removable lid supported by struts notched into the sides.

Detail from the corner of a building (right) showing the survival of timber baseplates on which walls were constructed.

The Walbrook streams needed continual maintenance and repair, something of paramount importance to the community due to the need for water and the ability to control it. Small footbridges allowed access across the roadside channels from the road into the buildings on the other side. One such footbridge led directly into a building, via a corridor that still had painted plaster upstanding on the walls on either side. Around AD 200 one section of the stream was infilled to make way for a new building. A backfilled stream does not seem the most logical location for a stable structure, which suggests that competition for space may have been such that any potential plot of land was utilised.

The buildings at Drapers' Gardens weren't without some Roman modern conveniences - many of the buildings also had associated box drains running alongside them, serving to drain off water from the eaves and clean, fresh water would have reached the City via simple aqueducts. This was piped into various buildings using pressure to move the water through oak log water mains pipes, with a bore of around 70mm. The pipes were split-out sections of large oak logs hewn very roughly square and joined by sharp tubular iron collars hammered into the end grain of each section. In one case a flanged lead spout leading up into the building was found still attached to the pipe with iron nails. The boring of wooden water pipes was another new woodworking technology introduced by the Romans to Britain and this site had the best-preserved sections of water main yet found in Roman London.

Within the rooms small tile hearths marked areas of domestic activity as distinct from the larger-scale industrial activities described above. Most buildings had rough beaten earth floors, which would have needed continual repair and alterations. However, one building had a timber planked floor and another had a floor of *opus signinum*, a type of hard pink concrete composed of crushed brick and tile mixed with mortar: an innovation brought in to London by the Romans during the second century.

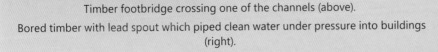
Timber footbridge crossing one of the channels (above).
Bored timber with lead spout which piped clean water under pressure into buildings (right).

Timber floor *in situ* seen from the west.

A second-century, single roomed, timber building found on site is one of the two best preserved ever found in London, the other being a timber framed and boarded sunken warehouse found in Southwark. Almost the whole plan of the building survived being rectangular and measuring *c.* 5.5m long and just under 4m wide.

The framework of the base of the building together with a timber-planked floor was found almost intact. The base of the wall survived on the south side and parts of what must have been the lime plaster and oak lathed ceiling was found lying on the floor.

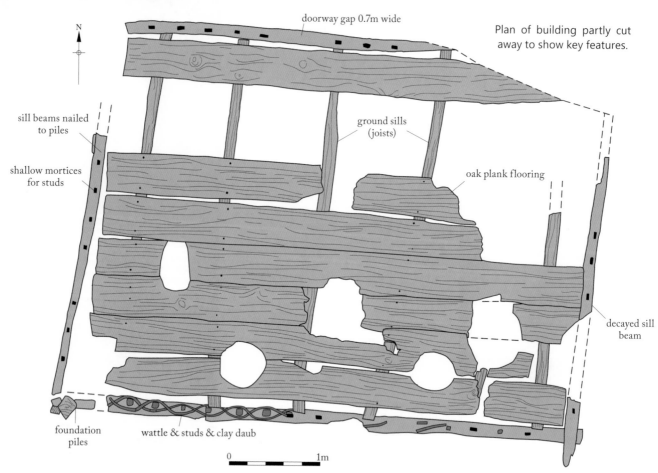

doorway gap 0.7m wide

Plan of building partly cut away to show key features.

N

sill beams nailed to piles

ground sills (joists)

shallow mortices for studs

oak plank flooring

decayed sill beam

foundation piles

wattle & studs & clay daub

0   1m

Research is ongoing and it is not yet clear what the building was used for. No hearth was found although the timber floor suggests that it was probably not just a store or workshop. It could, however, have been heated by a brazier, which would have left little trace.

The base frame was made of small oak logs hewn into rectangular beams joined at the corners with cross halvings. Shallow mortices were cut to hold the feet of oak poles hewn roughly square. These studs were set *c.* 0.3m apart and flexible stems *c.* 25mm in diameter woven horizontally around them and then plastered with clay (right). This is quite different to what is typically found in Roman London where wattle work is typically woven vertically around cross battens wedged between studs. Once the daub had dried the builders applied plaster to the surfaces. A *c.* 0.7m wide gap in the studs in the northern sill beam suggests that there was a doorway at that point.

The floor of the building also largely survived. It was originally made up of nine sawn oak planks nailed to small oak joists set directly on the ground. The planks were a 'cubit' *c.* 0.44m wide, a typical standardized Roman size.

A wood chip or bark layer lay over and around this curious little building, but whether it is a clue to the function of the structure is uncertain at this point.

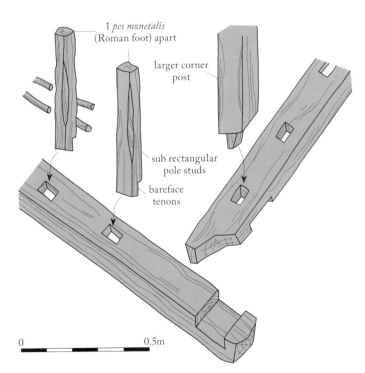

1 *pes monetalis* (Roman foot) apart

larger corner post

sub rectangular pole studs

bareface tenons

0   0.5m

Details of joins in sill beams at southeast corner of building.

The layouts of the various buildings on site evolved and changed from the mid second century through to the end of the third century. New buildings replaced the older ones and new structures were also erected in previously undeveloped locations. The nature of the structures remained constant however: industrial and craft activities continued to take place within these sparsely-furnished timber framed buildings. Between AD 120 and AD 300 five archaeologically identifiable 'phases' of buildings had existed on the Drapers' Gardens site. The evidence from these structures paints a picture of craftsmen and artisans working, trading and living in close proximity, a thriving community within the northern limits of *Londinium*.

A timber-framed building, complete with internal joists, constructed over the backfilled channel, during excavation (above).

Plan showing how the site had evolved by AD 250 (below).

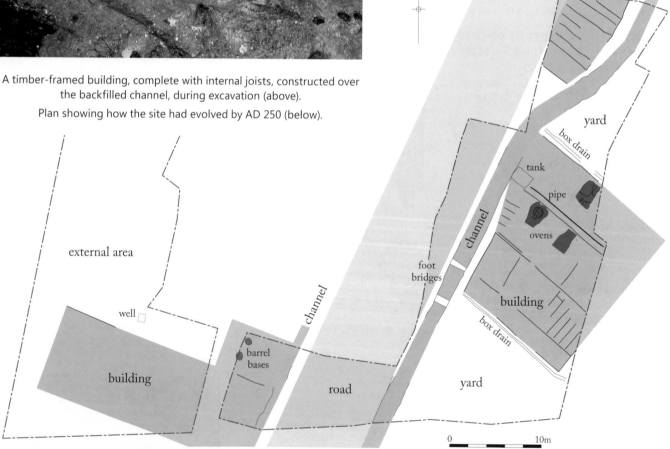

Excavating a fragment of mosaic flooring.

In-situ painted wall plaster was found on the timber fabric of the second- and third-century timber buildings (above right) and indicates that the interior of these buildings would have been embellished with some colour and patterning. Plain and decorated plaster that adorned the interior walls and ceilings of Roman dwellings does not often survive in the archaeological record, as it is a fragile lime-rich material that disintegrates readily. What is more the paint will normally bleach on exposure to weathering. Therefore the survival of 150kg of material (much of it painted in tones of red, black, blue, orange, green, yellow and pink) is a testament to the unique waterlogged conditions present at Drapers' Gardens and at other Roman sites that border the River Walbrook.

The survival of an *opus signinum* floor surface within one of the timber-framed buildings (see below) demonstrates the durability of this pioneer Roman concrete. Such surfaces are usually associated with higher status buildings, however overall the various Roman buildings at Drapers' Gardens were fairly low-status and similar to those excavated previously in the vicinity. What made this site so remarkable was the exceptional preservation and the sheer size of the area investigated. Almost an entire urban street and associated buildings spanning many years of the Roman occupation was uncovered.

29

Trade & industry

In the late first century AD the Roman historian Tacitus was to write that London was a city 'thronged with merchants and business men' and four hundred years later a Welsh monk could wistfully hark back to Roman Britain when luxuries used to come into Britain via the Thames, for Tacitus' merchants and businessmen relied on this river, which linked the city to the sea and allowed goods to be shipped into Britain from all corners of the Empire. *Londinium* was a trading centre through which luxuries, metals, foodstuffs, pottery, slaves and all manner of goods and chattels flowed on their way into and out of the province.

The site at Drapers' Gardens was in the middle of one of the noisiest and most industrial looking parts of the Roman City. In the late first and second centuries pottery kilns and glass furnaces located just off Moorgate would have sent clouds of acrid smoke and fumes over the cramped wooden dwellings. In yards butchers would have been slaughtering cattle. The meat from these abattoirs would have gone for sale, the bones for glue and the horns for working into all manner of objects. Carpenters would have been sawing and hammering, bakers were baking bread in wood fired ovens, traders were hawking their wares and weighing their produce for sale.

Roman currency in the first and second centuries was based on gold, silver and copper-alloy denominations, some of which were found at the site.

30

All types of dry goods were sold by weight. When lead weights like this are found it is a sure sign that commercial activities were taking place nearby.

Slaves would even have been rolling enormous barrels of wine off ox-carts newly arrived from the docks. Quantities were enormous and some of these luxury vintages from Gaul and Italy may have been decanted from their barrels and amphora into the little white flagons made by the nearby kilns for sale. Some of this wine was, no doubt, destined for the tables of the rich and wealthy, other rougher vintages for the fetid grog shops and tavernas of the city where it was drunk alongside locally made beer and mead. The Romans though wouldn't dream of drinking their wine neat and always drank it *mixtum* – mixed with water – only a barbarian would drink neat wine.

A copper-alloy finger-ring with a dark blue glass 'stone' engraved with a standing figure. Rings like this were cheaper versions of gold and silver ones and were used to seal documents.

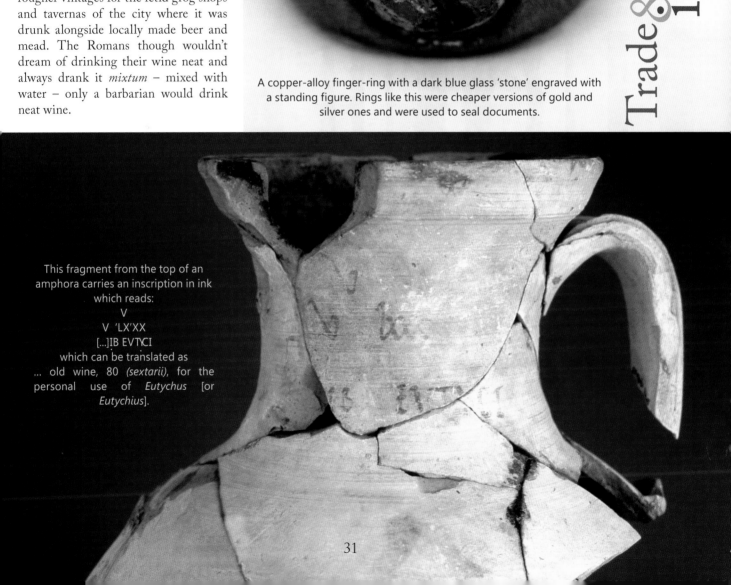

This fragment from the top of an amphora carries an inscription in ink which reads:

V

V 'LX'XX

[...]IB EVTYCI

which can be translated as

... old wine, 80 *(sextarii)*, for the personal use of *Eutychus* [or *Eutychius*].

31

The saw blades, clay ovens, weights, coins, wooden barrel staves, poleaxed cattle skulls, and shattered pottery cups are the detritus that remains from which we, as archaeologists, attempt to reconstruct this picture. Yet from these remains we can reconstruct the way the city's economy waxed and waned during the Roman period, from bustling commercial boom town in the first and second centuries to administrative centre in the fourth century. The coins even allow us to see how the Roman Empire's fiscal policies destabilised the economy in the third century. From such clues the economic history of *Londinium, Britannia* and the Roman Empire are reconstructed.

Several broken saw blades (above) were found which might have been used for cross cutting wood in a bow saw or 'serrata'. The finer toothed examples might have been used for bone.

Numerous punches were also found (left) and it is likely that some of these were used to drive nail heads flush with surface of timbers such as floor and wall cladding boards.

Five conjoining planks were found which formed the head of a wine barrel (only four are illustrated here). There are two stamps on this, maker's marks both made with the same brand: the full text reads *SEX SERVANDI* (the second brand has some letters missing) which stands for *Sexti Servandi* – the product of Sextius Servandus. Four graffiti are also visible here. It is not always possible to be certain what graffiti like this mean. One simply appears to be the letters CIP, perhaps someone's initials, a second reads *Capriacum*, possibly referring to a region of Burgundy from where the wine came. There is a scored out number 9 (*VIIII*), with a reversed C in front of it - perhaps a batch number. The numerals *CV XIS* probably refer to the volume of wine contained – this refers to two units of measurement the *sextarius* (precisely 0.547 litres, but a measurement close to our modern pint) and the modius (sixteen sextarii, or 8.754 litres, not far off two gallons). This barrel thus contained 105 *modii* and 11½ *sextarii*, or 925 litres of wine.

32

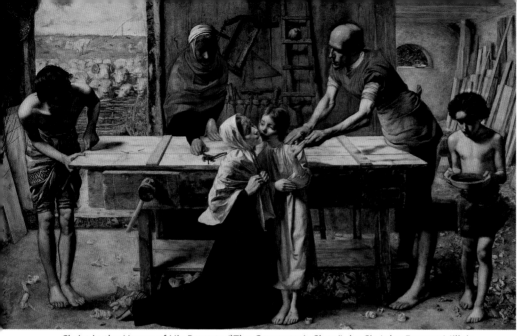

Christ in the House of His Parents ('The Carpenter's Shop'), by Sir John Everett Millais, a mid nineteenth-century view of a Roman carpenter.

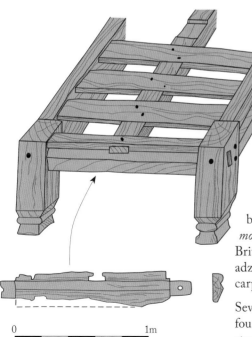

0   1m

Several important woodworking tools were also found during the excavations where conditions preserved metal work as well as woodwork.

The most important single tool found was the remains of a wooden ruler (right), an extremely unusual find since such items rarely survive. The ruler is probably of ash wood and was planed and then inch (*unciae*) divisions scribed on with the 3, 6, 8 and 10 inch marks further highlighted with compass marks. The ruler extends to *c.* 11.75 inches and seems to have been marked out to fit the common Roman *pes monetalis* foot which was just under an Imperial British foot. Other important tools include a broken adze hammer, the fundamental tool of the Roman carpenter, saw blade fragments and a bow drill bit.

Several small scraps of Roman joinery timbers were found dumped or reused, one piece that particularly stands out is a small jointed and moulded oak timber that was probably the end of a couch or bed (left).

33

Leatherwork only survives in very wet or very dry conditions. At Drapers' Gardens the former prevailed and there were some astonishingly well preserved pieces of leather. One of these (left) was decorated with gold. The gilding here is reminiscent of that seen on a pair of Roman period shoes from Egypt, preserved in the collections of the V&A.

Evidence for tanning (preparation of leather from hides) has been found slightly further north in the Walbrook Valley, but it appears that leather working may have been a principal industry here at Drapers' Gardens. Large quantities of leather were recovered from the excavations comprising fragments of shoes and sandals, including some for very small children, stitched pieces of leather and leather waste. The stitched leather included parts of garments, bags and pouches as well as possible tent panels. The leather working waste includes elements that suggest processing of animal carcasses on site to remove hides, such as the skin from an animal's head and two legs, as well as waste from working the tanned and prepared leather. Some of these trimmings and off-cuts of leather provide evidence that sandals were being made nearby, perhaps in one of the workshops beside the road.

Two sandals were found which have a very unusual double toe strap fixture (right).

The remains of five sandals founds at Drapers' Gardens (below). These range in size from a large adult to small child's shoe and, from left to right, equate to modern British shoe sizes 10 ½, 8 ½ and child's sizes 12, 8 and 8.

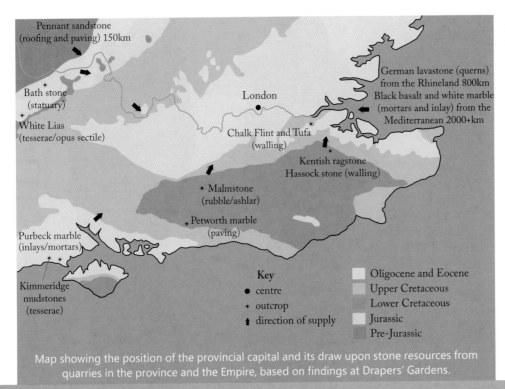

Pennant sandstone
(roofing and paving) 150km

Bath stone
(statuary)

White Lias
(tesserae/opus sectile)

London

German lavastone (querns)
from the Rhineland 800km
Black basalt and white marble
(mortars and inlay) from the
Mediterranean 2000+km

Chalk Flint and Tufa
(walling)

Kentish ragstone
Hassock stone (walling)

Malmstone
(rubble/ashlar)

Petworth marble
(paving)

Purbeck marble
(inlays/mortars)

Kimmeridge
mudstones
(tesserae)

Key
- centre
- outcrop
- direction of supply

Oligocene and Eocene
Upper Cretaceous
Lower Cretaceous
Jurassic
Pre-Jurassic

Map showing the position of the provincial capital and its draw upon stone resources from quarries in the province and the Empire, based on findings at Drapers' Gardens.

London lies in an area of the British Isles where much of the natural bedrock is too young and unconsolidated for fine carving. Yet the demand for stone to construct and embellish important Roman public and private buildings would have been at its greatest in the provincial capital. With this in mind, it would have been necessary to bring a whole range of stone types in from afar. The capital's excellent riverine and maritime position would have ensured a steady supply of limestone and sandstone from the west country via the River Thames and more exotic materials from the continent.

The findings from Drapers' Gardens reflect this, with a startling array of twenty different varieties of worked stone identified under the microscope.

Fine white limestones and hard dark grey dolomitic mudstones from Somerset and Dorset were present in the mosaic and *opus-sectile* flooring of the town houses.

36

Mortars, similar to those used in many kitchens today, and made of polished Purbeck marble from Dorset, Mediterranean white marble and black basalt were all found at Drapers' Gardens.

Much of this material came from the Roman consolidation dumps that line the River Walbrook (see pages 18–19) and does not appear to relate to the timber structures that lie alongside it. Instead, many of these carvings, inlays and mosaics would have once adorned the walling and flooring of an affluent masonry town houses in the Roman city. The inlays included triangular fragments of White Lias (right) which would have formed part of a decorative *opus-sectile* floor scheme, made from pieces of stone cut into different shapes to form an overall design. Shelly limestones from Dorset and West Sussex, such as Purbeck marble, were used in inlays to decorate walls.

37

Animal bone:
evidence for carcass preparation & craft activities

A butcher shown using a poleaxe in a woodcut by Jost Amman, 1568.

As with other waste materials found at the site animal bones were not removed to be disposed of away from dwellings, but were discarded close to where they were processed or consumed – dumped into disused pits and wells or thrown directly into the channels of the Walbrook.

The very large quantities of cattle bones found at this site, while obviously showing a fondness for beef, also provide evidence for various specialist activities, including those of butchers, bone workers, horn workers and glue makers. The initial stages in the butchery process are slaughter, skinning and dressing.

Until fairly recently in this country and indeed on the continent, the usual way to dispatch the larger domestic animals (cattle and horse) was by stunning followed by exsanguination (bleeding out). Prior to the modern age these animals were stunned using a particular butchers' tool, the poleaxe, which was essentially an axe with a hammer face opposite the blade. The method involved striking the animal, using the hammer face, in the middle of the forehead. Several sites in London dating from the Roman to post-medieval eras have provided cattle skulls with damage in the appropriate areas, clearly showing the antiquity of this method. Amongst numerous examples at Drapers' Gardens there is one skull fragment with a clearly visible rectangular indentation, an indication of the shape and size of the instrument used.

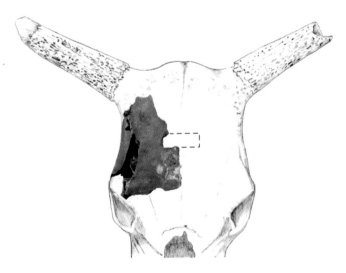

A cattle skull fragment dated to the second century with a rectangular indentation interpreted as poleaxe damage.

38

Second-century AD relief showing a Roman butcher using a cleaver.

After skinning, the butchered animal would be dressed, essentially the removal of the meat-poor parts (head and foot bones), producing the carcass often seen hanging up in butchers today. Dumps of bones largely composed of such parts are referred to as butchers' waste and almost certainly suggest the presence of butchers or even a butchers' market in the vicinity. Numerous examples were found at this site including a large collection from a fourth-century well, which provided at least 24 cattle skulls. This particular assemblage also produced a large proportion of vertebrae, shoulder blades and hip bones.

It has been noticed at other Roman sites in London that butchers' waste dumps tend to include these extra parts from third and fourth-century deposits. This may show a greater use of processed meat and certainly suggests an increase in the sale of meats taken off the bone. A frequently observed aspect of urban Roman butchery is the extensive use of the cleaver, including for the removal of meat from limb bones. This rather excessive butchery has been interpreted as the result of methods employed by professional butchers to speed up the processing of carcasses to meet the meat demands of the large city populace.

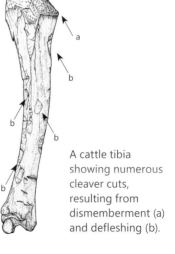

A cattle tibia showing numerous cleaver cuts, resulting from dismemberment (a) and defleshing (b).

The very large concentrations of cattle horncores found at this site could represent either hornworking or tanning waste. Both processes would have required waterproof pits, either clay and timber, or just clay-lined. The skins would require a lengthy soaking between layers of oak bark, while the removal of the horn sheaf (the useful part) from the bony core could be similarly achieved by soaking.

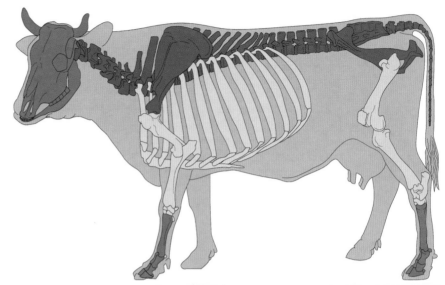

The skeletal parts which can be interpreted as butchers waste (right), including the head and foot bones (brown) and the additional parts (dark grey) found in second-century and later deposits.

Some of the many cattle horncores recovered at Drapers' Gardens (below).

Several ox-goads were found at the site. These would have been fixed to the end of a long stick, like a cattle prod, and used to round up or drove cattle or oxen. Here they may reflect cattle being brought to the site 'on the hoof'.

In the absence of such features, it could be supposed that the horncores signify hornworking waste, as the sheaf can be separated from the core by allowing the horn to rot in the open air.

Numerous fragments of leather were found at this site and indeed from other sites in this general area, but this is an indication of leather working rather than tanning. It is unfortunately very difficult to gauge the importance of horn as a raw material in Roman London as it rarely survives in archaeological deposits.

Similar accumulations of cattle horncores have been found at a number of sites in the vicinity, clearly suggesting the importance of hornworking or tanning, or a combination of both, in this part of the Roman City. Notably, greater concentrations have been recovered from late Roman levels, as indeed they were at Drapers' Gardens where out of a total of 1,500 horncores, 1,300 were from deposits dated to the fourth century.

As well as possible hornworking, there is ample evidence for glue manufacture, comprising large concentrations of heavily smashed cattle longbones, again dating from the second to the fourth centuries.

One or more open-air hearths found in the eastern part of the site may have been used to heat the vessels in which the bones were boiled, allowing the extraction of various oils and fats. Similar assemblages have been found at a number of contemporary sites in this area, a further indication of the generally industrial nature of this part of the Roman City.

Diet & environment

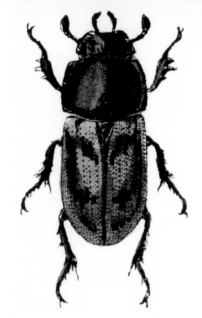

Archaeologists can learn much about ancient natural environments through examination of soil. During the excavations we recovered samples of sediment from archaeological features, including Roman wells and drains, essentially by digging out the soil and putting it directly into clean buckets. The soils were examined and described to record their colour and composition, including the amounts of gravel, sand, silt, clay, organic matter and artefacts they contained. This helps us to determine how the soils built up, whether they were deposited by water as part of a flood event, dumped as rubbish or brought into the site as hard core for example. However, the soils also contained biological remains, which had become preserved, or fossilised, by contact either with fire (charring) or by the waterlogged conditions prevalent at the site.

Examining these remains through a microscope allows us to identify pollen grains and spores, seeds, wood, charcoal and insects, which help to reconstruct a picture of the plants growing around the site, the diet of the inhabitants and the general environment at Drapers' Gardens.

From this we know that before any Roman occupation of the site there were shallow, muddy ponds, as well as rotting vegetation – the streams of the Walbrook flowing through this area were broad and slow-moving. Fossilised insect remains identified include species of water beetles that thrive in shallow ponds and drainage ditches (*Rhantus*) and shallow, muddy ponds (*Helophorus*) as well as a beetle (*Anotylus*) which thrives on rotting vegetation or carrion, where it preys on maggots.

This fossilized record of microscopic remains tells us that before this part of *Londinium* was occupied the area was covered in grassland. There were slow-running streams and stagnant muddy puddles, also areas of water meadows, with plants such as buttercups, fat hen, dandelions, mugwort, nettles, sedges

The preserved insect remains from the site included those of the beetle *Aphodius distinctus*, which feeds on cattle dung indicating that cattle were brought to the site 'on the hoof' for slaughter.

and grasses. Beech, hazel and oak trees all grew nearby and the presence of dung beetles tell us that animals roamed here too.

Although the area around Drapers' Gardens became intensively occupied and the streams of the Walbrook controlled and channelled, it was still not far from damp, mixed deciduous woodland, on the margins of streams and grassland, perhaps just beyond the city walls 100m or so north of the site. Here alder, hazel, holly, ash, willow, elm, pine and oak wood all grew. *Vincenzellus ruficollis*, a beetle that thrives on tree bark, tells us that hardwood trees such as hawthorn or beech stood nearby. The beetle species *Bembidion* suggests the presence of plants that live at the water's edge and *Chrysolina* feeds on herbs and shrubs and indicates upland meadows.

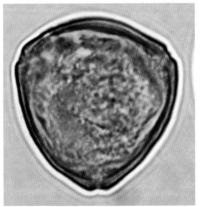

Hazel pollen, as seen through a high magnification microscope.

42

Very unusually at Drapers' Gardens backyard or wasteland trees growing *in situ* also survived and these trees can be firmly placed in the Roman cityscape alongside the buildings, roads and manmade structures. Nearly all the Roman timbers used in buildings on site were oak, however the forms of the trees and their sizes and growth rates can also tell us much about changes in environmental conditions, changes which find a parallel in the modern world. Early in the Roman period substantial timbers were used in construction, suggesting that stands of very large old oaks, or wildwood, covered much of the countryside. However, as time passed progressively smaller, faster-grown oaks were used, typical of trees growing in managed woodland cut repeatedly after a few decades. Having used up the abundant natural resources, the area became deforested and it was necessary to replant and manage the woodland around *Londinium*.

The presence of the grain pest *Oryzaephilus surinamensis* suggests that cereals were being stored close to the site.

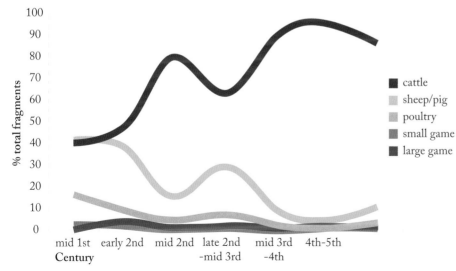

Representation of meat consumed throughout the Roman occupation period.

% total fragments

100 90 80 70 60 50 40 30 20 10 0

- cattle
- sheep/pig
- poultry
- small game
- large game

mid 1st   early 2nd   mid 2nd   late 2nd -mid 3rd   mid 3rd -4th   4th-5th

Century

The butchers' waste described above is a by-product of the consumption of animals and allows us to determine what was being consumed and how this varied over time. These animals fall into three main groups, namely domesticated animals (cattle, sheep and pigs), game and poultry. Throughout the occupation of the site, domesticates provide most of the bone with little evidence of the other food groups except during the first and early second centuries. Clearly there was a far greater usage of larger animals, particularly cattle, following the development of the site (the first buildings).

The second-century buildings were accompanied by large collections of bone waste from butchers and various crafts/industries which would not be expected in a site of higher status. The notable decline in the use of game and poultry on the site may also suggest a decline in status.

The fragments of amphorae recovered from the site, with their graffiti indicating producers, place of origin and quantities, suggest that wine was being imported in large amounts. This wine would have been drunk from pottery beakers and cups. Locally produced beer was also consumed. Studying the changing volume of these beakers shows that in the early Roman period beakers were small (for the consumption of wine) but by the late Roman period they were much bigger (for the consumption of beer).

Bread was the staple carbohydrate consumed by most of Roman Britain's inhabitants. In the countryside bread was made by individual house-holds and the flour was ground from locally grown grain. In the cities bakers produced bread for sale and at Drapers' Gardens the presence of two ovens located directly next to each other within one open room suggests the production of bread on a commercial scale. The bases of the ovens were made of tile and they most probably had domed superstructures though these did not survive.

These ovens were set directly on the floor of the building, but otherwise would have functioned much like a traditional pizza oven, where burning timber was placed within the dome. Once sufficient temperature was reached the hot embers would be raked to one side of the oven and the loaves placed inside to bake.

Detail of third-century mosaic from St-Romain-en-Gal showing a Roman bread oven in use (above). Base of an industrial-sized bread oven (left), one of two within a building range providing the fresh bread to the paying public. An iron bread shovel (right), used to take bread in and out of the ovens.

45

Literacy & writing

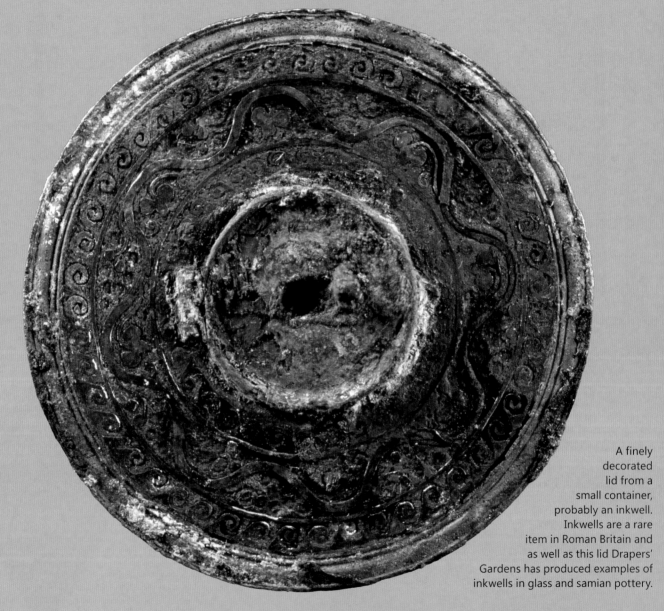

A finely decorated lid from a small container, probably an inkwell. Inkwells are a rare item in Roman Britain and as well as this lid Drapers' Gardens has produced examples of inkwells in glass and samian pottery.

A complete amphora top was found with an inscription deeply incised around its rim. The inscription reads: IANVARI K V MVIIIS which is an abbreviation of *Ianuari K̇V m(odios) VIII s(emis)* meaning '(Property) of *Januarius KV*, (capacity) eight (and) a half *modii*.' *Ianuarius* is quite a common name, so KV was presumably added to identify this particular individual; perhaps he was *Ku(piti filius)*, 'son of *Kupitus*' [*Cupitus*].

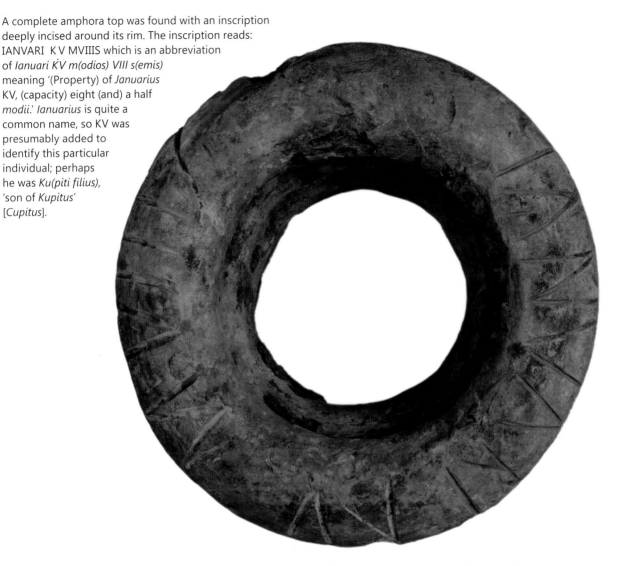

We take writing for granted. It surrounds us in our everyday lives: in the newspapers we read, the notes we scribble and the letters we receive. Yet in the early decades of the first century AD literacy was a new skill restricted to but a few people in Late Iron Age Britain.

The Roman conquest changed everything. Latin was both a spoken and written language. For us this means that Britain entered, for the first time, a historic epoch, and surviving histories and documents can aid our interpretation of the archaeological record.

For the inhabitants of Roman Britain writing offered unheard-of possibilities. A letter could be sent from Hadrian's wall to *Londinium* in a matter of days, lists of goods traded and exchanged could be drawn up, land could be bought and sold and documents could be produced to prove that the transaction had taken place.

The introduction of writing had created a new world and the Britons were quick to realise it.

Third-century relief detail of a man writing on tablets; from the so-called 'circus monument' from Neumagen, Germany. The relief depicts a commercial scene, probably the selling of goods and keeping accounts.

Leather was a valuable commodity used in huge quantities by both the civilian and military economies. This example is branded with the three initials T. F. B. possibly a tanner's mark to identify a hide or bundle of hides before tanning, or the initials of a supplier.

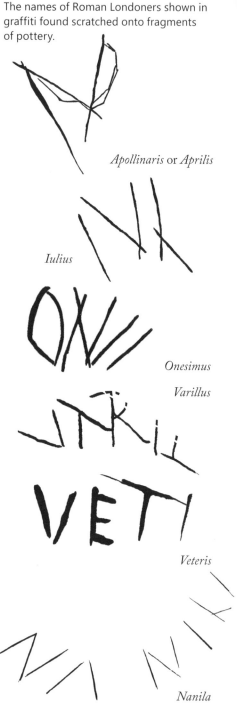

The names of Roman Londoners shown in graffiti found scratched onto fragments of pottery.

Apollinaris or *Aprilis*

Iulius

Onesimus

Varillus

Veteris

Nanila

Those engaged in washing, counting and weighing the 45,000 pieces of Roman pottery from the site remember with fondness the monotony of the task broken occasionally by the discovery of a piece of writing scratched on a fragment. Usually these words were the names of those Roman Londoners who owned the pot. *Apollinaris* or *Aprilis*, *Nanila*, *Onesimus*, *Veteris*, *Iulius* and *Varillus* were all people who at one time or another had lived or worked on the site. Sometimes the writing was a measurement of a vessel's capacity - showing that even *Londinium* had its trading standards officers!

London has produced many impressive Latin texts. Some of these are great monumental inscriptions but some are more humble, such as a wooden writing tablet from No.1 Poultry recording the purchase of the slave girl Fortunata for 600 *denarii*. The excavations at Drapers' Gardens have yielded nothing that compares with these inscriptions or texts. That said, what is clear from the excavations is that all sorts of people, including humble artisans and craftspeople, could and did write. For us their surviving words offer an unparalleled insight into the lives of *Londinium's* inhabitants.

Other evidence of writing came from the Roman equivalent of biros - styli – that were found across the site. The stylus is essentially a rod of metal with a pointed nib at one end and a flat 'eraser' at the other. These were used to scratch lists and notes into writing tablets. Many of the writing tablets from the site show where the sharp point of the styli cut through the soft wax and scored the wooden backing below.

Wall painting from Pompeii, showing a Roman lady with wax tablet and stylus.

Here a variety of styli and writing tablets show some of the types of writing equipment used at the site. Many of the tablets were used as 'note pads' with temporary notes scribed into soft wax held by the tablet's recesses. Sometimes faint scratches can be seen on the tablets when the writer pressed too hard, but none is legible.

49

The discovery of a number of inkwells, made from pottery, glass and metal, also shows that letters and documents were written in ink. Remarkably even pieces of leather, wooden barrels and pottery jars carrying wine were found with writing. Usually the text relates to the barrel or jar's contents or shows who manufactured the goods. The very ubiquity and casual use of writing shows how this skill had permeated all levels of Romano-British society. This is not to say that everyone was literate but there were probably more literate people in second-century *Londinium* than fifteenth-century London.

The late Roman period

Struck
in AD 310
at Trier, the
nine solidi Arras
Medallion depicts,
on the reverse, the
personification of London
kneeling before the city gate,
which is approached by a Roman
warship. Constantius is portrayed mounted
on horseback in the guise of a triumphant emperor,
holding a spear in one hand and a globe in the other, with the
inscription "restorer of eternal light." The earliest known depiction of London, this
medallion commemorates the restoration of Britain to the Empire after a period of instability.

Londinium in the late third and fourth centuries was a very different place to the bustling port and commercial boom town of the early Roman period. The third century had been a period of crisis for the Roman Empire. Civil war, invading barbarians along the Rhine-Danube frontier and an expansionist Persia in the east had been coupled with hyper-inflation and a near total collapse of the currency. Together these factors had brought the Empire to its knees.

By the early fourth century the empire had been stabilised and its borders restored - all of this was largely due to the efforts of a series of capable emperors. Britain, protected by the Channel, had escaped many of the third century's trials and tribulations. The broad and long-lasting social and economic changes that had swept the Roman Empire were felt though. Long distance trade declined, the rich grew more powerful while those of lower social status became ever-more oppressed and Britain's towns, caught up in this, went from being centres of production to places where resources were consumed.

Red jasper intaglio (or gemstone from a seal ring) showing a legionary eagle flanked by standards. This gem was probably cut in the mid-second century for a high ranking army officer and is one of the finest examples of its kind from Britain. It was found in a late fourth-century channel fill and must have been a very valuable antique when it was lost.

Late Roman *Londinium* was very different from its early Roman precursor. Huge defensive walls, still surviving here at Tower Hill, surrounded an important administrative centre but most industry was now located in the countryside.

What did all this mean for *Londinium* and Drapers' Gardens? Late Roman London was clearly still an important place. The city was surrounded by a substantial defensive wall and we know that it held a mint and a treasury during the fourth century and was the seat of the *Vicarius* (civilian governor) of the British provinces. Many substantial domestic buildings of this period have been excavated, but public buildings were falling into ruin or being demolished and some parts of the city were even being abandoned and reverting to open ground.

One of the great problems that face archaeologists working in London is the degree to which medieval and modern actions have removed evidence for earlier phases of activity. This has meant that the evidence for late Roman activity (being higher up and thus more likely to be destroyed) has always been partial and fragmentary.

At Drapers' Gardens the level of disturbance was surprisingly low but even so modern activity had basically planed off the layers and building remains of third- and fourth-century date. Compared to the wealth of structural evidence surviving from the early Roman period the late Roman phases look paltry. However, the scant traces that survived do tell an exciting story and one that is changing the way the Walbrook Valley is viewed in the late Roman period.

This plan of the latest Roman phase of activity shows how little survived destruction by modern construction. The channel shows the drainage system was being maintained but the wells indicate that the supply of piped, fresh water had failed.

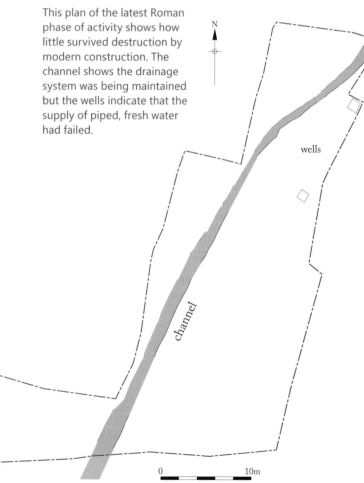

Carefully constructed timber-lined wells were the source of fresh drinking water for the site's fourth-century inhabitants. Though differing in construction detail these were generally made of oak planking and strengthened at opposing corners by bracing struts.

There are basically three types of late Roman feature that survived to be excavated and they had all been cut or driven into the underlying first- and second-century layers. Those features are wells, a substantial revetted channel running alongside the Roman street and the tips of timber posts. From these fragments of evidence a story can be told.

A total of four Roman timber-lined wells were found during the excavation, each subtly different in construction and all examples of solid cost conscious carpentry. The earliest second-century example only survived one course high with the sawn oak planks joined by single dovetails and iron nails. A well-lining (above) is typical of those known from Roman London made of sawn oak planks with two sets of corner struts and the corners jointed with single dovetails.

52

The two latest well-linings excavated on site included one which contained an exciting hoard of metalwork. The well-lining itself, however, was of interest being made in a most rustic way more typical of pre- or post-Roman times. The planking lining this well was made by splitting medium sized oak logs in half and axe trimming each half log to make a plank rather than by sawing. The return to this labour-intensive method in the fourth century suggests that there were disruptions in the supply of building materials to the City at this time. The well's corners were reinforced by diagonal struts built in which could also be used as a ladder for access. Each course was held in place by the rammed backfill and roundwood stakes driven in alongside.

Another well-lining found nearby had a different, stronger construction. It was made of sawn oak planks a standard 250mm wide and jointed at the corners with halvings and iron nails into the end grain. Unusually the nails were set in crude counter-sink holes and the heads covered by white mortar, a unique feature. At some point in the life of the well it was partly relined using planks of sawn poplar, a very rare example of the use of this soft deciduous wood for structural use in Roman London.

It has generally been assumed that during the fourth century environmental changes had caused the Walbrook Valley to flood and to revert to its marshy, pre-Roman nature. Much of our evidence suggests that this was not the case – at least in the Drapers' Gardens area.

The channel alongside the road was maintained, implying that the watercourse was still capable of being managed. The timber posts are probably all that remains of timber piles driven into the soft underlying layers to support late Roman buildings. Some of these may have been built in stone or been half-timbered as suggested by fragments of stone and tile from some of the late Roman features which may have been derived from buildings on the site. Finally, the use of wells as a source of fresh water shows that people were living on the site and implies that the early Roman piped water supply, presumably provided by a technically complex aqueduct system, had failed.

The finds from the roadside channel also shed much light on the site during the late Roman period. Large dumps of domestic and industrial waste were tipped into the channel and these dumps contained vast quantities of animal bone, pottery and other finds.

Most of the pottery in these channels was manufactured in Britain but little (if any) was made in London. Instead, kilns in Essex and Kent, Hampshire and Oxfordshire and even the Nene Valley and Dorset supplied most of the vessels used. Imports from the continent were much rarer but old samian vessels (from Gaul) and other finewares imported into Britain a century or more before survived as antiques. Amphorae, used to carry oil and wine, are also much less common. Less oil was being exported from Spain and less wine from Gaul. What few amphorae (and exotic contents) did reach the site came from the Tunisia and other sites around the Mediterranean. The inhabitants of fourth-century London were using fat and tallow instead of olive oil for cooking and lighting. Their drink,

Detail from inside corner of one of the wells, showing reinforcing struts which could be used as a ladder for access.

held in much larger drinking vessels, was now beer and mead rather than the exotic Mediterranean wines. Long-distance exchange was now much less intense and local produce and commodities were consumed instead of the rare traded luxuries of earlier times.

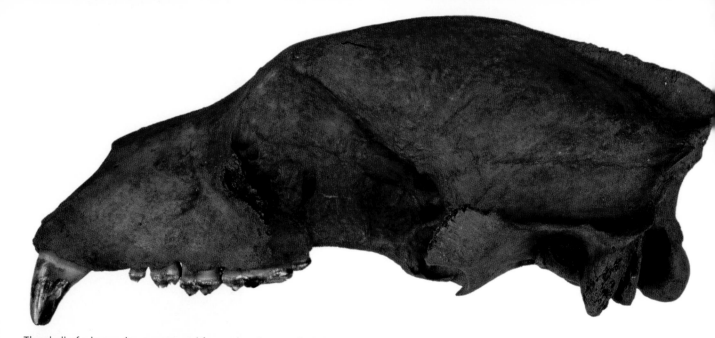

The skull of a brown bear recovered from a late Roman ditch fill. Note the well-worn teeth, which suggest an age between 8 and 20 years.

Detail of a mosaic from Leptis Magna, showing amphitheatre scenes.

A complete skull of an adult brown bear was found in one of the late Roman channels on the site, dated to the late fourth/early fifth centuries. This very unusual find represents only one of a total of three bear bones found in Roman London, each of the others also dating to the late Roman period. This species may well have died out in most parts of Britain by this time and could therefore represent the remains of an imported animal. One possibility is that this animal may have been used for entertainment, essentially for bear baiting, maybe in this area, or perhaps on a grander scale if it can be associated with the amphitheatre. There are vivid accounts of bear baiting and live hunting scenes at various Roman amphitheatres. One type of entertainment involved executions staged as re-enactments of stories from Greek mythology. Thus at the inaugural games at the Colosseum in Rome in AD 80 there was 'Orpheus devoured by a bear', 'Daedalus mangled by a bear' and in a rather loose translation of Prometheus and the eagle, a criminal was tied to a cross and ripped limb from limb by a 'Caledonian bear' *i.e.* a Scottish bear.

As the fourth-century progressed it became apparent that Britain was largely isolated from the centre of imperial power based at Trier (in modern-day Germany) , Milan or Ravenna (in Italy). In response to this Britain became the focus for a series of bids launched for the imperial throne by usurping generals based in Britain but they were all defeated. Reprisals after these usurpations were sometimes savage. People caught on the wrong side of the political fence could expect short shrift when legitimate imperial power was re-imposed. Worse, barbarian tribes had crossed the frontiers of the empire and a growing military crisis was unfolding. Britain, suffering at the hands of raids by the Picts, Scots and Saxons, was low on the list of imperial priorities. After yet another abortive bid for the imperial throne by an army officer in Britain in AD 407 imperial power was never restored and we enter the shadowy world of the fifth century and the 'Dark Ages'.

For the inhabitants of Drapers' Gardens these events may have had a great or tiny impact on their lives. We do not know whether anyone who lived on the site suffered at the hands of a raiding Saxon or lost their life or possessions in support of a usurper like Magnentius (the son of a Briton), Magnus Maximus or Constantine III. What we do know is that by the end of the fourth century life was beginning to change and one of the most surprising and startling finds from the excavations is an eloquent testimony of this and is the subject of the next chapter.

Picts, Scots and Saxons all raided Britain in the fourth century and these 'barbarian' peoples must have added to the instability of life in some quarters. There is little evidence that London suffered but many river estuaries in the South East were protected by the forts of the 'Saxon Shore'. This Anglo-Saxon burial from Eriswell in East Anglia shows the shape of the new Dark Age order: the pagan warrior buried with his sword and horse.

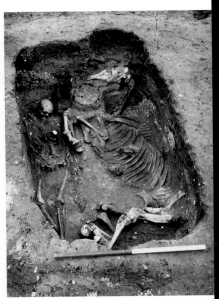

Magnentius was the son of a Romano-Briton and was proclaimed emperor in AD 350. He killed the legitimate emperor Constans in AD 351 but was defeated by Constantius II in AD 353. The Roman historian Ammianus Marcellinus records that savage reprisals were undertaken in Britain against Magnentius' supporters. Many wealthy Romano-Britons may have suffered as a result of this.

The hoard

The most startling discovery was made on a Tuesday afternoon in August 2007. Christopher Jarrett – the Company's medieval pottery specialist – had drawn the short straw and was excavating the bottom of a timber-lined well. It was nasty work, cramped and muddy with filthy water seeping through the well's side – a job few would relish. But at about 2pm Chris saw something gleaming dully through the murky water and soon realised he had found a copper-alloy vessel.

The hoard as a collection of objects immediately after it was excavated and before conservation. This image gives a good idea of the hoard's physical size.

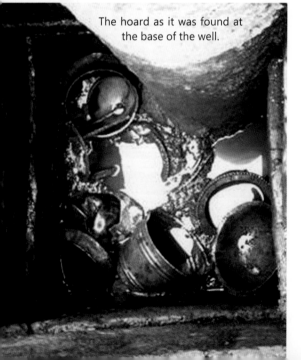

The hoard as it was found at the base of the well.

As he bailed water and muck from the well's base more and more of these vessels emerged. He had found the Drapers' Gardens hoard - a discovery of international importance.

The hoard totalled twenty metal vessels manufactured from copper-alloy, pewter and iron. There were bowls and buckets and ladles and jugs and even an iron trivet (right). By the time each of these vessels had been recorded and lifted from the well they filled the back of a Transit van. Few of us on site had ever seen anything like it and we realised pretty quickly that this was a very special find.

56

A frenzy of activity ensued, every object was photographed as it was when it came out of the ground, initial cleaning was kept to a minimum and a detailed drawing was made of each item before it went off for conservation. This process ensured that the vessels were stabilised - having spent around 1600 years buried in the damp environment of the well their sudden exposure to air might badly affect their condition - and then painstakingly restored to bring them as much as possible back to their original state (above left).

Shortly after this came a press release and details of the find were broadcast. The Drapers' Gardens site hit the headlines and the hoard went on temporary display at the Museum of London (below left).

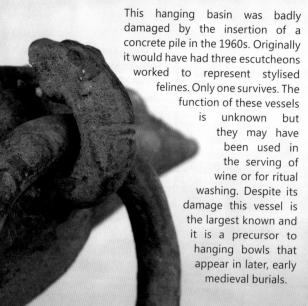

The hanging bowl from the seventh-century ship burial at Sutton Hoo (above, with detail below). In the fifth to ninth centuries hanging bowls may have been produced by British metalworkers and are often found in Anglo-Saxon burials. The most famous example is this one from the kingly grave at Sutton Hoo. Others are decorated with Christian motifs suggesting they may have been used in Christian liturgy.

This hanging basin was badly damaged by the insertion of a concrete pile in the 1960s. Originally it would have had three escutcheons worked to represent stylised felines. Only one survives. The function of these vessels is unknown but they may have been used in the serving of wine or for ritual washing. Despite its damage this vessel is the largest known and it is a precursor to hanging bowls that appear in later, early medieval burials.

Unravelling the hoard's story took a little longer. One of the first things that was established about the hoard was its approximate date. From the silt below the hoard were two Roman coins. Both were struck for the emperor Gratian at Constantia in southern Gaul (Arles in S. France) no earlier than the year AD 375. The hoard was above these coins and must have been placed in the well after them so the hoard can be no earlier than this date. As Roman rule in Britain came to an end around AD 410, it was clear that this extraordinary collection of copper-alloy vessels must date to the closing years of London's life as a Roman city.

Two bronze nummi of the Emperor Gratian. Struck at Arles in southern France, they show that the hoard cannot have been placed before AD 375. They are also the first element in the series of actions that included the placing of the hoard in the well.

'Perlrandbecken' or pearl edged bowls. A typical late Roman metal dish style. The hoard contained a variety of dishes and some may have been intended as 'nested' serving sets.

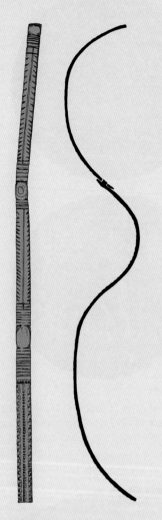

The deliberately bent copper-alloy bracelet. Evidence from cemetery sites suggests bracelets like this were worn by young women. Its bending may have been intended to 'kill' the object as part of a ritual in which it was dedicated to the gods.

When it was realised that the hoard dated to so very late in the Roman period it seemed easy to explain why it had been placed in the bottom of a well. It seemed obvious to assume that it had been hidden by some fairly well off inhabitants of Roman London during a time of danger. That they never returned to collect their expensive tableware seemed an eloquent testimony to the insecurity of late fourth-century Britain. Further analysis of the finds demonstrated that things were not so straightforward.

For some time now archaeologists have been aware that wells and springs were venerated as special 'religious' places during the Roman period. The great temple complex built around the hot springs at Bath is the best known example of this. At Drapers' Gardens the first clue that the hoard had been deposited as part of some elaborate religious ceremony came from two finds recovered from just above where the coins were found and below the first metal vessel. These finds were an iron bucket binding and copper-alloy bracelet. The binding had clearly been forcefully removed from the bucket and the bracelet had been broken and then carefully bent into an 'S' shape. This sort of deliberate damage is typical of finds made during the excavation of temple sites and is known as 'ritual killing'. It is thought that when objects were dedicated to the gods they were deliberately damaged as part of the ceremony.

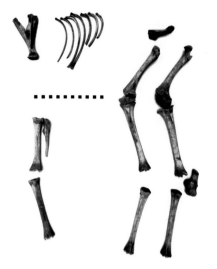

The pitiful remains of a very young red deer (above). Was this animal hunted outside of *Londinium's* walls as part of an elaborate ritual? Why were the skull and spine missing? Was the head struck off and set atop a wooden post as part of a religious ritual?

The distribution of red deer bones from the well superimposed onto a drawing of the skeleton of a young deer (below).

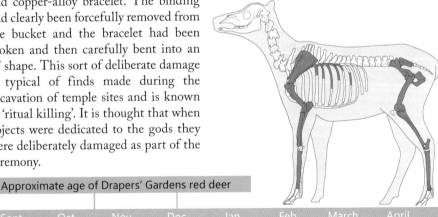

Approximate age of Drapers' Gardens red deer

May	June	July	August	Sept	Oct	Nov	Dec	Jan	Feb	March	April
	Offspring produced		Young weaned. Adult antlers fully grown	The Rut							Young separated from parents. Antlers begin to grow

Fragment of a mosaic from East Coker, Somerset, showing two men returning from a hunt with a stag.

The next piece of evidence that indicated that the hoard had probably been deposited as a religious act was identified some months after the excavations had finished.

In a bag of bones collected from the well were a few scraps of sheep and cattle – waste typical of many of the deposits on the site. However, there was also a collection of tiny bones that (to an expert eye) were all that remained of parts of the carcass of a red deer no more than 5 to 6 months old. The deer skeleton included most of the leg bones and a few ribs. It is possible that a few bones were lost during excavation (young bones tend to be quite fragile), but this wouldn't explain the absence of the head and all the vertebrae. A better explanation is that the carcass had been disarticulated prior to burial and that only certain parts were deposited in the well.

It is assumed that this animal was deposited into the well as some kind of offering, following the hoard. Now this raises three questions. Why did they choose red deer? Why such a young animal? And why didn't they use the whole carcass? There are no clear answers to these questions but certain inferences can be made based on comparable finds. Partial animal remains are commonly found as grave goods in Roman cemeteries, although these tend to be domesticates, such as pig and chicken, rather than game species.

The recovery of deer remains in a recognisably 'ritual' deposit is rare, with just two other published examples. These include an arrangement of deer, horse and dog skeletons, all complete, in a pit associated with the nearby Roman East London cemeteries and two semi-complete skeletons in the lower fill of a well at Baldock in Hertfordshire. They all date to the late Roman period and each is aged between 5 and 6 months.

61

Copper-alloy skillet (above).

A large cauldron (below) known as a 'Westland' cauldron because so many have been found in the Westland region of Sweden. It may have been produced in Britain or in northern Gaul.

The large bucket (right) is a rare and highly unusual object that is difficult to parallel. It is too fine to have been used for drawing water from the well. A similar example comes from a fifth-century grave in Nubia (Egypt/Sudan) and raises the possibility that it might be a product of a centre like Constantinople, Antioch or Alexandria in the eastern Mediterranean.

We can never know the exact reasons why the hoard was buried but we can reconstruct how it was deposited. Firstly, the coins were placed in the well, then the bucket that drew water from the well was dismantled and the binding dropped in. This was followed, probably by a young woman, removing one of her most personal possessions – the bracelet – and carefully bending it before dropping it too down the well. There may also have been a feast and the metal vessels could have been used in its preparation and display. Their placing in the well seems to have been undertaken with some care. The great hanging basin went in first and then the other vessels on top in little stacks. Some dirt was shovelled over the hoard and finally the partially dismembered carcass of the deer was placed in the well shaft. Its age suggests that these events may have taken place in autumn or winter, though it could have been as late in the year as midwinter. A connection with a major religious festival like the autumnal equinox or the feast of Samhain (summer's end) is a tempting possibility but cannot be proven.

The deposition of the hoard in the well marked the end of the Roman period at Drapers' Gardens. The well was now out of use and clean fresh water was no longer available. We can only speculate, but perhaps it was meant to appease the deities of the Walbrook and secure good fortune for its owners as they embarked on a new life elsewhere, as the Western Roman Empire teetered and then fell in the early years of the fifth century.

Pewter jug. Drinking vessels were absent in the hoard but this little pewter jug suggests the consumption of wine. The West Country was a centre of pewter production in the fourth century but the raw materials (lead and tin) were mined in Britain and were widely traded, so this may be the product of a local pewterer.

Medieval & later

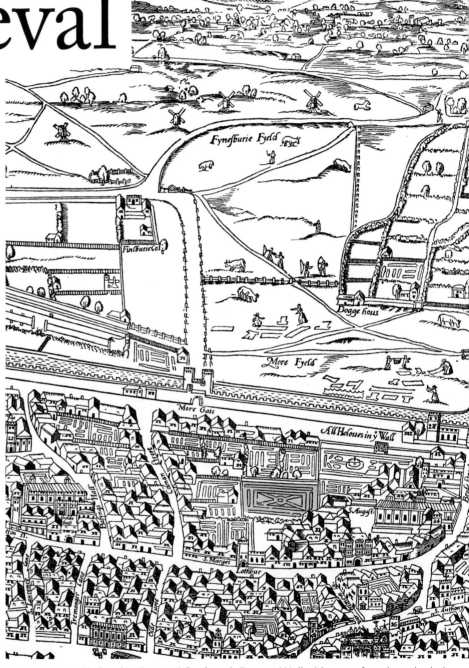

Following the fall of the Roman Empire at the beginning of the fifth century AD the old walled city was largely deserted for over 400 years. The Anglo-Saxons preferred to live upstream in the Covent Garden/Strand area in a settlement known as *Lundenwic*. It was only after a series of devastating raids by new invaders, the Vikings in 841, 851 and 871, that King Alfred initiated a return to the old Roman city in 886, renovating the old city defences to provide protection against the new menace. At first reoccupation of the city was largely confined to the riverside area centred on Queenhithe. The upper Walbrook valley with its meandering streams and tributaries had been allowed to return to its natural courses since the Roman water management fell into disuse. A large marsh was formed outside the city walls at Moorfields, which covered much of the northern area outside the city defences. Within the city the wide shallow valley of the Walbrook also became waterlogged. It was thus one of the last parts of the settlement within the walls to be built upon and indeed much of the immediate area of the site remained outside the urban spread of the new and bustling medieval city because of its uninviting, wet environment.

Agas Map c. 1562 showing Drapers' Gardens & Drapers' Hall with area of gardens shaded.

There was very little survival of medieval or later archaeological remains on site, in part due to the fact that the basements of the late nineteenth- and twentieth-century buildings had removed late Roman and later deposits, especially on the western part of the site. Additionally, however, the area had been unattractive for settlement because of its marshy nature, which led to it being turned over to gardens for much of the post-medieval period (AD 1485 onwards). No longer confined within the Roman timber revetments, the Walbrook reverted to a wider course some 6m across. During the late twelfth century the channel was lined with timber planks and a fence separated the river from a building to the east. This structure may represent the furthest encroachment of the medieval urban settlement northwards into the marshy area.

Medieval flint-tempered greyware storage jar or cooking pot from south Hertfordshire, dated 1170-1350. The rim has two finger impressions, either from the potter handling the jar roughly after he had finished throwing it or possibly as batch marks.

The only evidence of post-medieval activity was a well lined with a reused timber barrel (below), which went out of use in the second half of the seventeenth century and may have been associated with the formal Drapers' Gardens.

A rectangular brass coin weight dating from the late fifteenth to early sixteenth century. This tiny weight measures only 14mm by 16mm and would have been used to test the weight of a particular gold coin, the 'noble'.

Drapers' Hall & gardens

UNTO GOD ONLY BE HONOUR AND GLORY

The Drapers' Company's first royal Charter is dated 1364, although an informal association of Drapers undoubtedly existed earlier. Indeed, the Company is said to have been in existence as early as 1180. The medieval Company monopolized and regulated the cloth trade within the City of London, setting prices and quality standards, overseeing the draper apprenticeships and managing and caring for those working in or retired from the trade.

Today the Company has wide-ranging interests and responsibilities. Whilst its earlier involvement in the woollen cloth trade has long ceased, the essence of the medieval fraternity has remained constant in the traditions of good fellowship, friendship, trustworthiness and charity. Its principal role today is the investment of its endowment and the trusteeship of its charitable trusts which give financial support to the relief of need, education and almshouses, together with the modern equivalent of its ancient trade, technical textiles. It extends hospitality in its Hall allowing substantial numbers of the general public to enjoy the splendour of the building, as well as providing extra resources to enhance the Company's capacity to further its charitable work. It continues to support the City of London Corporation and Mayoralty not only through the electoral system but also in such instances as supporting the Lord Mayor's charity and overseas scholarship scheme.

Drawn by Tho. H. Shepherd.   Engraved by W. Watkins.

DRAPERS' HALL, THROGMORTON ST.

As the English woollen cloth trade expanded in the fifteenth century more people became involved in the trade and with the Company, resulting in the need for a Hall where members could meet to discuss and co-ordinate business. Initially individuals' houses were used, but in the 1420s the Drapers decided to build their own Hall in St Swithin's Lane.

The present Hall, situated in Throgmorton Street, was bought from King Henry VIII in 1543. This had been the house of Thomas Cromwell, Earl of Essex and Chief Minister to the King, but had been forfeited to the Crown on Cromwell's arrest and execution in July 1540. The Hall was entirely destroyed in the Great Fire of 1666. It was re-built, and again seriously damaged by fire in 1772, since when it has from time to time been reconstructed and altered into its present form.

The original Drapers' Hall had been built for Thomas Cromwell on land previously occupied by small tenements. Unhappy with only a 'reasonable' plot of land for his garden, Cromwell ordered the fences of the surrounding gardens to be taken down and a high brick wall to be erected, again this was done without prior notification to the owners of the gardens.

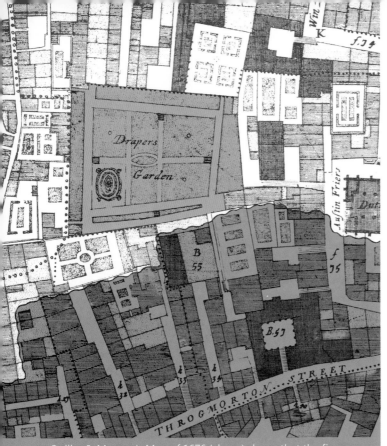

John Stow's father had a house and garden nearby and Stow tells us of his father's surprise at finding, with no warning, that the neighbouring house had been lifted up, set on rollers and moved into his garden, to make way for Cromwell's grand garden. When Stow's father spoke to the surveyors about this, their response was "that their master Sir Thomas commanded them so to do" and he notes that "no man durst go to argue the matter, but each man lost his land, and my father paid his whole rent, which was 6s. 6d. the year, for that half which was left. Thus much of mine own knowledge have I thought good to note, that the sudden rising of some men causeth them in some matters to forget themselves".

The garden behind the Hall is a small proportion of the original garden attached to the Hall purchased by the Drapers' Company from King Henry VIII in 1543.

The Great Garden as it was originally called, is now occupied by the modern building known as Drapers' Gardens, but in 1543 this was where rose bushes, gooseberry trees, gourds, strawberries and herbs were planted. A bowling alley, a maze and summerhouses added to its attraction. Company archives reveal much detail as to how the gardens were planted and laid out.

Open to the public, the Great Garden was a welcome oasis in the City. Over the centuries rules and regulations were drawn up reflecting changing fashions and the increasing pressure on this valuable open space.

Ogilby & Morgan's Map of 1676 (above) shows that the fire was stopped just before the site, no doubt helped by the open space provided by the gardens. After the Great Fire the gardens were opened to the public, and soon became a fashionable promenade an hour before dinnertime.

The first Drapers' Hall, formerly Thomas Cromwell's mansion.

In the nineteenth century the garden was open every day except Sunday and rainy days 'for the recreation of genteel company' and was used for flower shows. However, the character of the City changed. Families were squeezed out by commercial pressure and the City became a place to work but not to live. This trend influenced the decision to build on the Great Garden and to slice Throgmorton Avenue through its east side in 1874.

By 1890 stockbrokers and jobbers were working in the buildings, which covered the Great Garden, interspersed with an occasional wine merchant and the Persian Consulate General. In 1966, a striking 30-storey concrete office block designed by Richard Seifert, took its place on the site. Whilst regarded in its day as an outstanding example of post-war design, the tower was no longer suitable for use as contemporary offices and its demolition was completed in November 2007.

The Ordnance Survey map of 1873 shows the Drapers' Hall and the Great Garden immediately before development.

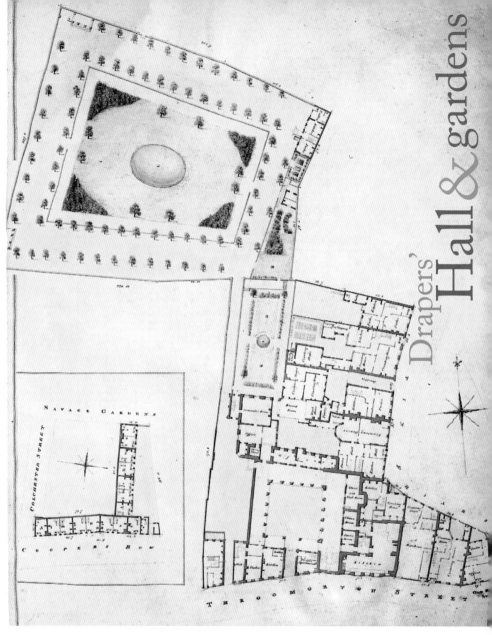

A survey of Drapers' Hall, its gardens and adjacent properties, dated 1819.

Drapers' Hall & gardens

The Great Garden was thus sacrificed to the demands of the commercial City, but the Upper Garden close to Drapers' Hall was retained, periodically renovated and flourishes today. The tradition of fruit bearing trees continues with the garden's five mulberry trees, of which one was planted by Her Majesty The Queen in 1955 and another by the Prince of Wales in 1971.

The new building

In 1999 the leaseholder and sole occupier of land at Drapers' Gardens, The Royal Bank of Scotland (RBS), was due to relocate from the 30-storey office tower and podium building that at that time stood on the site. Development options were considered by RBS in conjunction with their consultant team, which included multi-disciplinary practice Foggo Associates, as architects, engineers and quantity surveyors. Possibilities considered ranged from refurbishing and converting the tower to alternative uses through to its demolition and replacement with a new commercial office development. In 2006, Drapers' Gardens Unit Trust, with Omega Land as development managers, acquired the site and scheme from Royal Bank of Scotland.

The 1960s tower designed by Richard Seifert had historical architectural and engineering interest, being a precursor to Centre Point and the Nat West Tower.

However, it had become obsolete in its use and was decaying structurally, so conversion to other uses proved to be unviable.

In May 2006, a 15 month demolition contract commenced, with Keltbray Limited carrying out the works, overseen by Foggo Associates, and Pre-Construct Archaeology undertaking excavation work. In addition to the logistical challenges of demolishing the tallest habitable building yet to have been demolished in the UK, the contract included the removal of the 3m-thick solid reinforced concrete raft foundation; broken with the controlled use of explosives, following the completion of the archaeological works. Sir Robert McAlpine were appointed as main contractor for the new building in December 2006, working alongside the design team to procure the various sub-contract works, prior to taking occupation of the site. Piling works started following completion of the demolition works, in October 2007. At the beginning of 2007, Canary Wharf Limited replaced Omega Land as Development Managers as well as becoming a joint investor in the scheme with Exemplar Developments LLP.

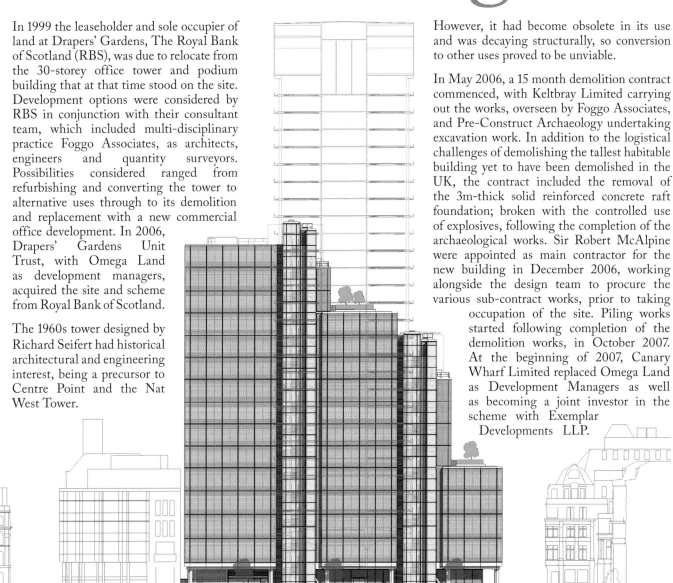

New Drapers' Gardens building elevation and previous tower profile.

The new building is designed to provide high-quality office accommodation whilst being flexible and environmentally responsive. The overall height of the new building was established in close consultation with the City of London planning department, with respect to various views; in particular that of the dome of St Paul's Cathedral from the centre of Waterloo Bridge. In this view the top of the new building is set at a level below the base of the dome of St Paul's, so that the visual profile of the Cathedral is not compromised, as it had been with the previous much taller tower.

Similarly, local street level viewpoints from within the Bank Conservation Area (in which the site is located) were considered. In discussion with the planning authority, a height limit sympathetic to the adjacent buildings along Throgmorton Avenue was established and the distinctive profile of the new building was developed, rising from 5-storeys on the east to the equivalent of 15-storeys on the west.

The landscaped roof terraces enhance the outlook from the building and can be used by the building's occupants. These aerial gardens have an historic affinity with the Drapers' Gardens site's history. The main building is due to be completed, ready for tenant fit-out to commence at the end of 2009.

The new Drapers' Gardens building.

The new building

The landscaped roof terrace.

The new building from the Drapers' Company livery hall garden.

Acknowledgements

Pre-Construct Archaeology Ltd would like to thank Exemplar Developments LLP and Canary Wharf Developments for funding the archaeological investigation. Special thanks are extended to Andrew Heath-Richardson and Andrew Proctor of Canary Wharf Limited, Tony Taylor and David Spencer of Foggo Associates, Nick Smith and Anthony Walsh of Keltbray for their help during the project. Thanks also to the City of London Planning and Transportation Committee for the approval of the scheme to develop the site, with particular thanks to Peter Wynne Rees, the City Planning Officer, Archie Galloway OBE, who as Broad Street Ward Common Councillor throughout the majority of the development has been supportive of the scheme from day one and to Alderman, Sir David Lewis MA, DL for his support as Ward Alderman for Broad Street and his contribution in the foreword of this publication.

Thanks are due to the Drapers' Company for their assistance during the excavation and in particular to David Addis and Penny Fussell for their assistance in providing text and images for this publication and making available a copy of the accompanying DVD. Thanks to Tim Hinton of Foggo Associates for his help in providing text and images for the final chapter of this book.

Pre-Construct Archaeology would also like to thank Kathryn Stubbs, Senior Archaeological and Planning Officer of the City of London, for monitoring the archaeological work. Thanks to Jane Sidell, English Heritage Scientific Adviser, for advice and guidance regarding the environmental strategy on site. Thanks also go to the archaeological consultants Mike Hutchinson and Pete Mills of Mills Whipp Partnership for their help and advice during both the archaeological works and the post-excavation process.

Neil Hawkins would like to thank the onsite contractors at Keltbray for their generous assistance and cooperation, in particular Nick Smith, Joe Allison and John Mitchell.

Many thanks to Jenny Hall and Francis Grew of the Museum of London for all their advice and help with the hoard and for providing images for use in this publication. Also thanks to Roger Tomlin, Quita Mould, John Shepherd and Ellie Leary for providing information on the graffiti, leatherwork, glass and human remains respectively. The tree-ring study of Ian Tyers was essential for the dating of the timber structures. Many thanks to Hannah Ridgeway for her invaluable help reading and commenting on drafts of this text.

Finally none of this would have been possible without the hard work and dedication of the excavation team, the finds manager Märit Gaimster, Robert Nicholson and all the finds processing crew.

Select bibliography

Barton, N., 1962, *The Lost Rivers of London.*

Blurton, T.R., 1977, Excavations at Angel Court, Walbrook, 1974, *LAMAS* 28, 14-100.

Clark, J., Cotton, J., Hall, J., Sherris, R. and Swain, H. (eds.), 2008, *Londinium and Beyond: Essays on Roman London and its hinterland for Harvey Sheldon*, CBA Research Report 156.

Drummond-Murray, J. and Liddle, J., 2003, Medieval Industry in the Walbrook Valley, *London Archaeologist*, Vol 10, No. 4, 87-94.

Gerrard, J., forthcoming, The Drapers' Gardens Hoard: a preliminary account, *Britannia.*

Gerrard, J., forthcoming, Wells and beliefs systems at the End of Roman Britain: a case study from Roman London. In L. Lavan (ed.) *The Archaeology of Late Antique Paganism.* Leiden, Brill Late Antique Archaeology 6.

Grimes, W.F., 1968, *The Excavation of Roman and Medieval London*, Routledge.

Hawkins, N., 2009, New evidence of Roman settlement along the Walbrook: excavations at Drapers' Gardens, *London Archaeologist*, Vol. 12, No.6.

Hawkins, N., 2009, *An Assessment of an Archaeological Excavation and Watching Brief at Drapers' Gardens, City of London, London EC2*, Pre-Construct Archaeology unpublished report.

Hawkins, N., Brown, G. and Butler, J., 2008, Drapers' Gardens, *British Archaeology 98*, 12-17.

Hawkins, N. and Butler, J., 2008, The Drapers' Gardens Roman Hoard, *Minerva* 19 No. 6, 47-48.

Maloney, C., with de Moulins, D., 1990, *The Archaeology of Roman London Volume 1: The Upper Walbrook in the Roman period*, CBA Research Report 69.

Marsden, P., 1980, *Roman London*, Thames and Hudson.

Merrifield, R., 1965, *The Roman City of London*, Ernest Benn.

Merrifield, R., 1983, *London City of the Romans*, Batsford.

Milne, G., 1995, *Roman London*, Batsford.

Perring, D., 1991, *Roman London*, Seaby.

RCHM, 1928, *Royal Commission on Historical Monuments, Vol.III: Roman London*, HMSO.

Rielly, K., 2008, The Drapers' Gardens Bear, *London Archaeologist* Vol. 11, No. 12, 318.

Schofield, J. with Maloney, C. (eds.), 1998, *Archaeology in the City of London: a Guide to Records of Excavations by the Museum of London*, Museum of London.

Seeley, F. and Drummond-Murray, J., 2005, *Roman pottery production in the Walbrook valley: Excavations at 20-28 Moorgate, City of London, 1998-2000*, MoLAS Monograph 25.

Stow, J., 1598, *A Survey of London.*

Weinreb, B. and Hibbert, C. (eds.), 1983, *The London Encyclopaedia*, Macmillan.

Wilmott, A., 1991, *Excavations in the Middle Walbrook Valley*, LAMAS Special Paper 13.

Picture credits

Pre-Construct Archaeology is grateful to the following for supplying and giving permission to reproduce images on the pages indicated:

Jenny Hall/Museum of London: The Drapers' Gardens display at the Museum of London, prelims & page 57; copper alloy vessels and escutcheon, prelims; 'Perlrandbecken' or pearl edged bowls, prelims & page 59; cauldron, bucket and ladle, page 62; pewter jug, page 63; pewter jug handle detail, page 75

Keltbray Limited: Building demolition and archaeology, page 1 & facing

Steve Duncan: The Walbrook Sewer, page 2

Museum of London: Head of Mithras, page 3; reconstruction of Roman London AD 60, page 8; relief of Mithras slaying the Astral Bull, the Copthall bowl, page 14; Tabard Square inscription, page 16

City of London, London metropolitan archives: Excavations at the Coal Exchange, City of London, page 5; the Drapers' Hall, page 69; Agas map of London, page 66; Ordnance Survey map of 1873, page 71

Colchester Museum: The Colchester Sphinx, page 17

Jake Lunt-Davies: Reconstruction of a Roman street scene at Drapers' Gardens, pages 20–21; depositing the hoard in the well, pages 64–65

The Tate: Millais' Christ in the House of his Parents, page 33

Victoria and Albert Museum: Gilded leather shoes, page 34

The Bridgeman Art Library: Relief of butcher using a cleaver, page 39; mosaic showing a Roman oven in use, page 45

Trier Landesmuseum: Relief of man writing on tablets, pages 48 & 76

British Museum: Arras Medallion, page 50; Sutton Hoo hanging bowl and detail, page 58

Suffolk County Council Archaeological Service ©: Saxon burial from Eriswell, page 55

The Guardian 2007© Guardian News and Media: Day-to-day relics reveal Roman London, page 57

The Daily Telegraph 2007© Telegraph Media Group Limited: Unearthed after 1,600 years, dinner set hidden by fleeing Romans, page 57

Somerset County Council Heritage Service: East Coker mosaic fragment, page 61

The Drapers' Company: The Upper Garden and Drapers' Hall, the Drapers' coat of arms, page 68; the first Drapers' Hall, page 70; a survey of Drapers' Hall, its gardens and adjacent properties, dated 1819, page 71

Foggo associates: Elevation of new building and tower profile, page 72

Miller Hare: The new building, pages 73 & 74

Fragment of mid to late second-century fineware jug from Central Gaul, showing figure of nude male.

Images on preceding pages:

75   Detail of handle of pewter jug, part of the fourth-century hoard of objects found in a well.
76   Third-century relief detail of a man writing on tablets.
78   Detail of Trajan's column, showing palisade construction.
79   The sole of a Roman shoe with hobnails.